HOW NOT TO BE A
PROFESSIONAL
FOOTBALLER
PAUL MERSON

HOW NOT TO BE A
PROFESSIONAL
FOOTBALLER

PAUL MERSON

with Matt Allen

HarperSport
An Imprint of HarperCollins*Publishers*

Published in 2012 by
HarperSport
an imprint of HarperCollinsPublishers
77-85 Fulham Palace Road,
Hammersmith, London W6 8JB

www.harpercollins.co.uk

First published in hardback 2011

1 3 5 7 9 10 8 6 4 2

A catalogue record of this book is
available from the British Library

ISBN 978-0-00-742497-9

Printed and bound in Great Britain by
Clays Ltd, St Ives plc

FSC™ is a non-profit international organisation established to promote
the responsible management of the world's forests. Products carrying the
FSC label are independently certified to assure consumers that they come
from forests that are managed to meet the social, economic and
ecological needs of present and future generations.

Find out more about HarperCollins and the environment at
www.harpercollins.co.uk/green

Contents

A Note from the Author

One thing before we crack on: an apology. You'll only hear it from me on this one page because I've read too many life stories and books where people are constantly tripping over themselves to make up for all the bad things they've done. Page after page after page of it, and after a while it just doesn't ring true.

The thing is, you're going to read a lot of bad things over the following pages, and some of it is pretty shocking. The last thing you need to get through is a million and one apologies as well, so you're only reading the one, but it's sincere. For the terrible things I've done and to some of the people I've hurt and let down: I'm sorry.

INTRODUCTION

Last Knockings

I'll tell you how bad it got for me. At my lowest point as a gambler, the night before an away game for Aston Villa, I sat on the edge of my bed in a Bolton hotel room and thought about breaking my own fingers. I was that desperate not to pick up the phone and dial in another bet. At that time in my life I'd blown around seven million quid with the bookies and I wanted so badly to stop, but I just couldn't – the next punt was always too tempting. Slamming my own fingers in a door or breaking them one by one with a hammer was the only way I knew of ending the cycle. It was insanity really. The walls had started closing in on me.

When I was bang on the cocaine, I sold my Arsenal blazer to a dealer because I'd run out of money in the pub and I was desperate to get high. All the lads at Highbury had an official club jacket, tailored, with the team crest emblazoned on the front. It was a badge of honour really, something the directors, coaching staff and players wore with pride. It said to everyone else: 'Being an Arsenal player is something special.' It meant nothing to me, though, not at my most desperate. I was out of pocket and there wasn't a cashpoint around, so I swapped it for one pathetic gram, worth just £50. The next day I told Arsenal's gaffer, George Graham, that the blazer had been nicked out of the back of my car. Well, at that stage in my life a made-up story like that seemed more realistic than the truth.

At the peak of my game, I was drinking more lager tops than the fans. I would go out three, four, five nights a week and drink pints and pints and pints, usually until I couldn't drink any more. Some nights I wouldn't go home. I'd leave training, go on the lash, fall asleep in the bar or finish my last beer at silly o'clock. Before I knew it, I was in a taxi on my way to training, then I'd go through the whole cycle all over again. Unless I'd been nicked, that is.

That happened once or twice. One night, I remember going into the boozer for a few beers and a game of pool with a mate. We got plastered. While we were playing, some lads kept having a go at us, shouting across the bar and making wisecracks, probably because they recognised me. This mate of mine was a bit of a wild card, I never knew how he was going to react when he was pissed. This time he blew up with a pool cue. A chair was thrown through the window; he smashed up the optics. It all kicked off and there was blood everywhere. The bar looked like a scene from a Chuck Norris film.

We ran home. I was covered in claret, so I chucked my shirt in the washing machine, turned it on and went to bed. That was my drunk logic at work: I thought the problem would magically disappear if I stuck my head under the covers. I even ignored my now ex-wife, Lorraine, who was standing there, staring at me, wondering what the hell was going on as I pretended to be asleep. It wasn't long before the police started banging on the front door. Lorraine let them in, and when they steamed into the bedroom, I made out they'd woken me up.

'Ooh, all right officer,' I groaned, rubbing my bloodshot eyes. 'What's the matter?'

The copper wasn't falling for it. 'Get up, you fucking idiot. You're under arrest.'

I was off the rails, but in those days I could get away with it most of the time. There were no camera phones or random drugs tests and footballers weren't followed by the paparazzi 24/7, which was a shame for them because they would have loved me today.

I was an England international and I played for some massive clubs. I made my Arsenal debut in 1986 and retired from playing 20 years later. In the course of my Highbury career I won two League titles (1989, 1991), an FA Cup (1993), a League Cup (1993) and a UEFA Cup Winners' Cup (1994). I won the Division One title with

How Not To Be a Professional Footballer

Portsmouth in 2003 and got promotion to the Premiership with Middlesbrough in 1998. I played in the last FA Cup Final at the old Wembley with Villa. I was capped for England 21 times, scoring three goals. I had a pretty good CV.

Off the pitch I was a nightmare, battling with drinking, drugging and betting addictions. I went into rehab in 1994 for coke, compulsive gambling and boozing. There were newspaper stories of punch-ups and club bans; divorces and huge, huge debts. I was a headline writer's dream, a football manager's nightmare, but I lived to tell the tale, which as you'll learn was a bloody miracle.

Through all of that, playing football was a release for me. My managers knew it, my team-mates knew it and, most of the time, the supporters knew it, too. Wherever I went, whoever I played for or against, the fans were always great to me. Well, maybe not at Spurs, but I got a good reception at most grounds – I still do. I think the people behind the goals watching the game looked at me and thought, 'He's like us.' I lived the life they did. A lot of them liked to drink and have a bet, and some of them might have even taken drugs at one point in their lives. They all thought the same thing about me: 'He plays football for a living, but he's a normal bloke.' They were right, I was a normal bloke and that was my biggest problem. I was just a lad from a council estate who liked a lorryload of pints and a laugh. I didn't know how to live any other way, and I had to learn a lot of hard lessons during my career because drinking and football didn't mix – they still don't.

All of my pissed-up messes are here in this book for you to read, so if you're a budding football superstar you'll soon know what not to do when you start out as a professional player. Treat this book as a manual on how to avoid ballsing it up, because every chapter here is a lesson. The rest of you will have a bloody good laugh, I hope, while picking up some stories to tell your mates down the boozer. Go ahead, I'm not embarrassed about my cock-ups, because the rickets made me the bloke I am today and the truth is, everyone cocks up now and then. My biggest problem was that I cocked up more than most.

LESSON
1

Do Not Go to Stringfellows with Charlie Nicholas

'Where Merse lays the first bet, reads his rehab diary and gets a taste of the playboy lifestyle.'

It was the beginning of the end: my first blow-out as a big-time gambler. There I was, a 16-year-old kid on the YTS scheme at Arsenal with a cheque for £100 in my hand – a whole oner, all mine. That probably sounds like peanuts for a footballer with a top-flight club today, but in 1984 this was a full month's pay for me and I'd never seen that amount of money in my life, not all at once anyway. Mate, I thought I'd hit the Big Time.

It was the last Friday of the month. I'd just finished training and done all the usual chores that you have to do when you're a kid at a big football club, like cleaning the baths and toilets at Highbury and sweeping out the dressing-rooms for the first-team game the next day. When that was done, Pat Rice, the youth team coach, came round and gave all the kids a little brown envelope. Our first payslips were inside, and I couldn't wait to draw my wages out. I got changed out of my tracksuit and ran down the road to Barclays Bank in Finsbury Park with my mate, Wes Reid. I swear I was shaking as the girl behind the counter passed over the notes.

'What are you doing now, Wes?' I asked, as we both counted out the crisp fivers and tenners. I was bouncing around like a little kid.

'I'm going across the road to William Hill,' he said. 'Fancy it?'

That's where it all went fucking wrong. I'd never been in a bookies before, but I was never one to turn down a bit of mischief. I wish I'd known then what I know now, because Wes's offer was the moment where it all went pear for me. The next 15 minutes would blow up the rest of my life, like a match to a stick of dynamite.

'Yeah, why not?' I said.

It was the wrong answer, and I could have easily said no because it wasn't like Wes was pushy or anything. In next to no time, I'd blown my whole monthly pay on the horses and my oner was down the toilet. I think I did my money in 15 minutes, I'm not sure. I'd never had a bet in my life before. It's a right blur when I think about it. I left the shop in a daze. Moments earlier I'd been Billy Big Time, but in a flash I was brassic. All I could think was, 'What the fuck have I done?'

At first I felt sick about the money, I wanted to cry, and then I realised Mum and Dad would kill me for spunking the cash. As I walked down the high street, I promised myself it would never happen again. I also reckoned I could talk my way out of trouble when Mum started asking all the questions she was definitely going to ask, like:

'Why are you asking for lunch money when you've just been paid?'

'Why can't you afford to go out with your mates?'

'What have you done with that hundred quid Arsenal gave you?'

At that time, Mum was getting £140 from the club for putting me up at home, which was technically digs. She'd want to know why I was mysteriously skint, or not blowing my money on Madness records or Fred Perry jumpers. There was no way I was going to tell her that I'd handed it all to a bookie, she would have gone mental. As I got nearer to Northolt, where we lived, I worked out a fail-safe porkie: I was going to make out I'd been mugged on the train.

Arsenal had given me a travel pass, which meant I could get back to our council-estate house no problem. The only hitch was my face. I looked as fresh as a daisy – there were no bruises or cuts. Mum wasn't going to believe I'd been given a kicking by some burly blokes, so as I got around the corner from home, I sneaked down a little alleyway and smashed my face against the wall. The stone cut up my skin and grazed my cheeks, and I was bleeding as I ran through our front door, laying it on thick about some big geezers, a fight and the stolen money. They fell for it, what with my face being in a right state, and I was off the hook.

Nobody asked any questions as Dad patched up the scratches and cuts, and the police were never called. Later, Mum gave me the £140 paid to her by Arsenal. I thought I'd been a genius. My quick thinking had led to a proper result, but I couldn't have guessed that it was the first lie in a million, each one covering up my growing betting habit.

As I went to sleep that night, I told myself another lie, almost as quickly as I'd told the first.

'Never again, mate,' I said. 'Never again.'

Ten years after the bookies in Finsbury Park, I went into rehab at the Marchwood Priory Hospital in Southampton. Booze, coke and gambling had all beaten me up, one by one. I never did anything by halves, least of all chasing a buzz, but I was on my knees at the age of 26. That first flutter had started a gambling addiction I still carry today.

Do Not Go to Stringfellows with Charlie Nicholas

As part of the treatment, doctors asked me to write a childhood autobiography as I sat in my room. I think it was supposed to take me back to a time before the addictions kicked in, to help get my head straight. I've still got the notes at home, written out on sheets of lined A4 paper. When I read those pages now, it seems my only real addiction as a lad was football, and that made me sick, too.

I was such a nervous kid that I used to wet the bed. I had a speech impediment, which meant I couldn't pronounce my S's, and I had to go through special tuition to sort it out. When I started playing football I'd get so anxious that I'd freak out in the middle of school games. God knows where it came from, but I used to get palpitations during Sunday League matches and I couldn't breathe. My heart would pound at a million miles an hour, and the manager would have to sub me because I thought I was dying. Mum and Dad took me to our local GP for help, and once I realised the pounding heart and breathing problems were only panic attacks and that they passed pretty quickly, I calmed down a bit.

I was a good schoolboy player, turning out for Brent Schools District Under-11s even though I was a year younger than everyone else. When I was 14, I was spotted playing for my Sunday morning side, Kingsbury's Forest United, and scouts from Arsenal, Chelsea, QPR and Watford wanted me to train with them. I went down to Watford, where I saw Kenny Jackett and Nigel Callaghan play (they were Watford players, if you hadn't sussed), and I went to Arsenal as well. I thought I'd have more of a chance of making it at Watford because of my size – I figured a small lad like me would have more hope of getting into the first team there – but my dad was an Arsenal fan, so I did it for him. In April 1982, I signed at Highbury on associated schoolboy forms, which meant I couldn't sign for anyone else until I was 16.

The chances of me becoming a pro were pretty slim, though. I had the skills for sure, I was sharp, quick-witted and I scored a lot of goals as a youth team player, but I was double skinny and Arsenal's coaches were worried that I might not be big enough to make it as a striker in the First Division. I definitely wasn't brave. When I played in games, I was terrified of my own shadow. It only needed a big, ugly centre-half to give me a whack in the first five minutes of a match for me to think, 'Ooh, don't do that, thank you very much,' and I'd disappear for the rest of the game, bottling the fifty-fifty tackles.

Don Howe was the manager at Highbury, and he was pushing me about too, but it was for the best. He'd spotted the flaws in my game and wanted me to toughen up. In 1984 he called me into his office, took a look at my bony, tiny frame and said, 'I'm not making you an apprentice, son, but I am going to put you on the YTS scheme. We get one YTS place from the government, so I have to take a gamble and I'm taking the gamble on you.'

Do Not Go to Stringfellows with Charlie Nicholas

There was a hitch, though. 'If you don't get any bigger, we won't be signing you as a professional,' he said, looking proper serious.

I didn't care, I was made up. I prayed to God that I'd fill out. I stuffed my face with food and pumped weights during the week like a mini Rocky Balboa.

In a way, getting a YTS place was like Charlie finding the golden ticket to Willy Wonka's Chocolate Factory, because it was a bit of a lottery really. Any one of a dozen kids at the club could have got that spot, but they gave it to me. The YTS players in Division One were also a bonus ball for the youth system. The government paid my wages (that oner a month), so it wasn't like the club had to fork out any cash for me. In the meantime, I was playing football and handing cash back to Maggie Thatcher in gambling taxes. Happy days all round.

But I still moaned. Being a YTS or apprentice player was a pain in the arse at times and I had to travel across London from Northolt to Highbury. Every morning without fail I'd get on the underground for 16 stops to Holborn, then I'd change to the Piccadilly Line and go the last stretch to the club. I lost count of the times I had to get off at Marble Arch to go to the loo. I had to run up the escalators of the station, nip into the khazi at McDonalds and then run back for another train.

Once I got to the ground, I'd help the other apprentices put the kit on the coach. We'd then drive 50 minutes into the countryside, train for a couple of hours and come back home again. I was constantly knackered. On the way home I'd always fall asleep on the tube. Luckily for me, Northolt was only a few stops from the end of the Central Line, so if I fell akip and woke up in West Ruislip, I didn't have far to travel back.

It didn't get much better for me when it came to playing football either. Because of my size I was never getting picked for the team and I was always sub. Sometimes I even had to run the line. During a pre-season game against Man United I was lino for the whole match and I had the hump, big-time. It didn't help that my mates were getting £150 a week for working on a building site when I was only get £25.

My attitude was bad. I kept thinking, 'I ain't going to make it as a footballer. I'm not even playing now. What chance have I got?' At that point I would have strolled over to the nearest construction foreman and said, 'Give us a job', but my dad kept saying the same thing to me again and again: 'Keep on going.' The truth is, I could have packed it in 50 times over.

Arsenal weren't much of a team to look at then. When I watched them play at Highbury, which the kids had to every other Saturday, they weren't very good. They had some great players around like Pat Jennings in goal, plus internationals like Viv Anderson, Kenny Sansom, Paul Mariner, Graham Rix and Charlie Nicholas, but Don couldn't get them going. They were getting beat left, right and centre and the fans weren't interested. These days, Arsenal tickets are as rare as rocking horse shit. In 1985, that team was playing in front of crowds of only 18,000.

At the same time, I started getting physically bigger and tougher in the tackles, which was a shock for everyone because my mum and dad were small. Suddenly I could look over the heads of the other fans on the North Bank. In matches I started being able to read the game, and I became what the coaches would call 'intelligent' on the pitch. Off it I was a nightmare, but when I was playing I was able to see the game unfolding in front of me. I could picture where players would be running and where chances would be coming from next, which a lot of other footballers didn't. And I was lucky, very lucky, because I didn't get injured.

See, this is the thing that people don't tell kids about professional football: it's so much down to luck, it's scary. If you don't play well in that first district game, the scout from QPR or Charlton isn't coming back. If you get injured in your first youth team match at Wolves and miss seven months of action, chances are, you're not getting signed. I was lucky because I avoided the serious knocks. My only bad injury came when I ripped my knee open on a piece of metal when I was 12 years old (before I'd joined Arsenal), and that now seems like a massive stroke of luck when I think about it.

How Not To Be a Professional Footballer

I was playing football with my mates on some park land at the back of our house in Northolt. I was stuck in goal and as a ball came across I rushed out for it, quick as you like, sliding across the turf. The council were still building around the estate then, and there was rubble and crap everywhere. A piece of metal wire sticking in the ground snagged the skin on my knee and tore it right down to the bone.

It was touch and go whether I'd play football again. The doctors gave me a Robocop knee with 30 stitches on the inside, another 30 on the outside. With medical science, they pieced me together with catgut, the wire they used in John McEnroe's tennis rackets. It gave my right leg some kind of super strength. After that I never had to use my left peg, because I could kick the ball so well with the outside of my right thanks to the extra support in my knee. When I was at Villa, our French winger David Ginola said to me, 'You are zee best I 'av ever seen at kicking with the outside of your foot, Merz.' That's some compliment coming from a great player like David, I can tell you.

As a trainee at Arsenal, I had the odd twisted ankle, a few bruises, but that was it. And then things started happening for me in the youth team. It took about seven months, but as I got bigger I became a regular in the starting line-up. I was scoring goals and playing well, while the lads in the year above me, like Michael Thomas, David Rocastle, Martin Hayes and Tony Adams, started playing in the reserves, knocking on the first-team door. I was offered a second year on my YTS contract and began training with the first team shortly afterwards. It was Big Boy stuff, but I really fancied my chances of getting a proper game. I even dreamt of watching myself on *Match of the Day*.

Then I made it into the reserve team. Once a youth footballer gets to that stage in his career, it can get pretty brutal. The pressure is really on to get a pro contract. Players are often chasing a place in the first-team squad with another apprentice, someone who could be their best mate. I spent a lot of time worrying whether I was going to make it or not, and it got to me. The panic attacks came back. During a reserve game against Chelsea I latched on to a through ball and rounded their keeper Peter Bonetti, who I'd loved as a kid because I was a Chelsea fan (though Ray Wilkins was my idol). But as I was about to poke it home, I got the fear and froze like a training cone. A defender nicked the ball off me and I was left there, looking like a right wally, feeling sick. A few days later I went to the doctors again, but the GP was like a fish up a tree. He told me to give up football, but I wasn't going to do that. I loved the game too much.

At training I managed to hold it together, which was a relief because I was playing with some proper superstars. Charlie Nicholas was one of them and he was a god to the Arsenal fans. He'd come down from Celtic, where he'd smashed every goalscoring record going. Graham Rix was there too, as was Tony Woodcock and top England centre-forward Paul Mariner, who was a player and a half. It was a massive deal for me. I remember being on the training ground and thinking, 'My God, these people are legends.'

The biggest shock was that they were all so normal. None of them were big-time, none of them were Jack-the-lads. It was a help, because I was a normal bloke too. I was determined never to become a flash Harry, which was probably what got me into trouble in the long run, and I could never say no to my mates at home. I'd already smoked weed in the park with them, but I'd packed it in when I signed Don Howe's YTS contract. I liked it because it relaxed me, but it gave me the munchies. I'd always end the night at the counter of a 24-hour petrol station buying bars of chocolate and packets of crisps, which wasn't the best for someone with an ambition to make it in the First Division.

I also liked a drink, which was something I was better suited to than grass. I found that the more I drank, the fewer panic attacks I'd have. I started in my early teens, knocking back the Pernod and black with mates, which was always colourful when it came back up. It didn't put me off, though. If my mum and dad went out on a Saturday night they'd often come back and find me passed out on the sofa, surrounded by a dozen empty cans of lager.

Do Not Go to Stringfellows with Charlie Nicholas

I suppose it was good training. After I'd been working with the first team for a while, Charlie Nicholas and Graham Rix took me under their wing, but this time it was off the pitch as well as on it. They had showed me the ropes at the club and told me how to handle myself during games, and then they invited me to Stringfellows in London, a fancy footballers' hang-out in the West End. My eyes were on stalks when I walked in for the first time, there were birds everywhere and they all wanted to meet Charlie. He had the long hair, the earring and the leather trousers. He was a football superstar, like George Best had been in the seventies.

'Fuck, I like this,' I thought. 'I want to be like him.'

This was at a time long before Stringfellows became a strip club, but it might as well have been one. The girls were wearing next to nothing and there were bottles of bubbly everywhere. Tears for Fears and Howard Jones blasted out from the speakers. I looked like the character Garth from *Wayne's World* because my eyes kept locking on to every passing set of pins like heat-seeking radar, and I couldn't believe the amount of booze that was flying around. Graham Rix's bar bill would have put my gambling binge with Wes to shame.

I crashed round at Charlie's house afterwards, a fancy apartment in Highgate with an open-plan living-room and kitchen, plush furniture, the works. I wanted all of it. Luckily, the club had decided to sign me as a pro, and I couldn't scribble my name down quick enough because there was nothing more I wanted in the world than to be a professional footballer. And I fancied another night in Stringfellows.

I got my contract on 1 December 1985 and at the time I thought it was big bucks, all £150 of it a week. Oh my God, I thought I'd made it, even though I was earning the same amount of dough as my mates on the building site. That didn't stop me from celebrating. I remember going round to my girlfriend Lorraine's house with a bottle of Moët because I reckoned I was on top of the world. The first-team players had given me a sniff of the high life available to a top-drawer footballer, and how could I not be sucked in by the glamour? I'd tasted bubbles with Champagne Charlie before we'd shared half-time oranges.

Arsenal were having a 'mare in 1986. Don resigned after a lorryload of shocking results, and George Graham turned up in May. I was gutted for Don. He was a top coach, one of the best in the world at the time. I worked with him again when he was looking after the England Under-19s, and he was phenomenal, really thorough and full of ideas. When he talked, you listened, but Don's problem was that he didn't have it in him to be a manager. Really, he was just too nice.

Do Not Go to Stringfellows with Charlie Nicholas

As a coach he was perfect, a good cop to a manager's bad cop. If a manager had bollocked the team and torn a strip off someone, I imagine Don would have put his arm around them afterwards. He would have got their head straight.

'Now don't you worry about it, son,' he'd say. 'The gaffer doesn't really think you're a useless, lazy fuckwit, he just reckons you should track back a bit more.'

Being a coach and a manager are two very different jobs. When someone's a coach they take the lads training, but they don't have the added pressure of picking the team or running the side, and that makes a massive difference. I don't think Don could hack that. He wasn't the only one, there have been loads of great, great coaches who couldn't do it as a manager. Brian Kidd was a good example. He was figured to be one of the best coaches in the game when he worked alongside Fergie at United. He went to Blackburn as gaffer and took them down.

Our new manager, George Graham, was a mystery to me. I didn't know him from Adam, apart from the fact that he was an Arsenal boy and he wanted to rule the club in a strict style. I'd heard he'd been a bit casual as a player. Some of the lads reckoned he liked a drink back in the day, and they used to call him Stroller at the club because he seemed so relaxed when he played, but when he turned up at training for the first time he seemed a bit tough to me. Straightaway, George packed me off to Brentford because he thought some first-team football with a lower league club would do me good. Frank McLintock, his old Arsenal mate, was in charge there and George was right, it did help, but only because we got so plastered on the coach journey from away games that some of the players would fall into the club car park when we finally arrived home. It prepared me for a lifetime of boozing.

I signed with Brentford on a Friday afternoon. Twenty-four hours later we played Port Vale, and what an eye-opener that was. To prepare for the game, striker Francis Joseph sat at the back of the bus, smoking a fag. We were comfortably beaten that afternoon and Frank McLintock was sacked on the coach on the way back. I thought, 'Nice one, the fella who's signed me has just been given the boot.' I couldn't believe it.

After that, though, it was plain sailing. Former Spurs captain Steve Perryman took over the club as player-manager and got us going. We didn't lose again, and after every game we celebrated hard. I remember we played away at Bolton in a midweek match, and when we got back to the dressing-room at 9.15, a couple of the lads didn't even get into the baths. They changed and ran out of the dressing-room so they could get to the off-licence before it closed. On the way home we all piled into a couple of crates of lager and got paro. It was a different way of life than at Arsenal. I learnt at Highbury that you could have a drink on the way home, but only if you'd done the business. At Brentford you could have a drink on the way home even if you hadn't played well.

Going to Brentford back then was probably the best thing that could have happened to me, because it made me appreciate Highbury even more. By looking at Brentford I could see that Arsenal was a phenomenal club. The marble halls at Highbury, the atmosphere, the way they looked after you was top, top class. I went everywhere in the world with them during my career. We played football in Malaysia, Miami, Australia and Singapore. When we played in South Africa a few years later, we were presented with a guest of honour before the match, a little black fella with grey hair. When he shook my hand, I nudged our full-back, Nigel Winterburn, who was standing next to me.

'Who the fuck's that?' I said.

Nige couldn't believe it.

'Bloody hell, Merse, it's Nelson Mandela,' he said. 'One of the most famous people in the world.'

I'm not being horrible, but I never got that treatment at Aston Villa. They were a big club and we might have gone to Scandinavia for a pre-season tour, or played in the Intertoto Cup, but it was hardly South Africa and a handshake from Nelson Mandela. I never got that at Boro or Pompey either, and I definitely didn't get that at Brentford. A couple of days after the Port Vale game, following my first day training there, I went into the dressing-rooms for a shower and chucked my kit on the floor. Steve Perryman picked it up and chucked it back at me.

'What are you doing?' he said. 'You've got to take that home and wash it.'

I couldn't believe it. At Arsenal, one of the kids would have done that for me. I'd train, get changed and the next day my kit would be back at the same place in the dressing-room, washed, ironed, folded up and smelling as fresh as Interflora, even though I didn't have a first-team game under my belt.

I loved it at Brentford and I was so grateful to them for starting my career. I go and watch them whenever I can, but I wasn't there for long as George soon called me back. Steve had wanted to keep me for a few more months, but I knew that getting recalled to Highbury so quickly meant one thing only. It was debut time.

I was right as well. I made my first appearance against Man City at home on 22 November 1986, coming on as a sub in a 3–0 win. I ran on to the pitch and all the fans were cheering and singing for me. Then with my first touch, a shocker, I put the ball into the North Bank. It was supposed to be a cross. Instead it went into Row Z. The Arsenal fans must have thought, 'What the fuck have we got here? This guy looks like a right Charlie.' They didn't know the half of it.

LESSON 2

Do Not Drink 15 Pints and Crash Your Car into a Lamppost

'Our teenage sensation drinks himself silly and gets arrested. Tony Adams wets the Merson sofa bed.'

That's when the boozing really started. Under George, I got to the fringes of the first team at the tail end of the 1986–87 season, and whenever I played at Highbury I'd always go into an Irish boozer around the corner from the ground afterwards. The Bank of Friendship it was called. In those days, my drinking partner was Niall Quinn, who had signed for the club a few years earlier. If you had said to me then when I was 17 or 18, 'Oh, Niall's going to be the chairman of Sunderland when he's 40-odd,' I'd have thought you were having a laugh. He wasn't that sort of bloke.

We'd often play games in the stiffs together, which took place in midweek. On the day of a match, we'd spend hours in the bookies before heading back to Niall's place for a spicy pizza, which was our regular pre-match meal. His house was a bomb site. I'd regularly walk into his living room and see six or seven blokes lying on the floor in sleeping bags.

'Who the fuck are these, Quinny?' I'd ask.

'Oh, I dunno. Just some lads who came over last night from Ireland.'

It was hardly chairman of the board material.

My Arsenal career had started with a few first-team games here, some second-string games there, but word was starting to spread about me. My life in the limelight had begun a season earlier in the 1985 Guinness Six-a-Side tournament, which was a midweek event in Manchester for the First Division's reserve team players and one or two promising kids. I loved it because the highlights were being shown on the telly.

We lost in the final but I was in form and picked up blinding reviews whenever I played. I was performing so well that the TV commentator Tony Gubba started banging on about me, saying I was a great prospect. Then Charlie Nicholas did a newspaper interview and claimed I was going to be the next Ian Rush. Suddenly the Arsenal fans were thinking, 'This kid must be good.' Everyone else wanted to know what all the fuss was about.

The only person who wasn't getting carried away was George. After my debut against City I had to wait until April 1987 before my first full game, and that was a baptism of fire because it was an away game against Wimbledon, or The Crazy Gang as most people liked to call them, they were that loony. In those days they intimidated teams at Plough Lane, their home ground. The dressing-rooms were pokey, and they'd play tricks like swapping the salt for sugar, or leaving logs in the loos, which never flushed properly. It annoyed the big teams like Arsenal who were used to luxury. Then they'd make sure the central heating was on full blast in the away room; that way the opposition always felt knackered before kick-off.

They were pretty hard on the pitch too. Vinnie Jones was their name player then, but Dennis Wise and John Fashanu could cause some damage. To be fair, they some-times played a bit of football if they fancied it, but that day we won 2-1 in an eventful game. Vinnie got sent off for smashing into Graham Rix, and I scored my first goal for Arsenal, a header. As it was going in, their midfielder Lawrie Sanchez tried to punch it away, but he only managed to push it into the top corner. I thought, 'The fucking cheek.'

I played in another four games as George eased me into the swing of things, but nobody else was handling me with kid gloves. In the next match I played against Man City again, this time at Maine Road, and when we kicked off I ran to the halfway line. I was watching the ball at the other end when City's centre-half, Mick McCarthy, smashed me right across the face. He didn't apologise but instead gave me a look that said, 'You come fucking near me again and I'll snap you in half.'

'No chance of that,' I thought. I hardly touched the ball afterwards.

George changed everything at Arsenal. In his first season, we won the 1986–87 Littlewoods Cup Final, beating Liverpool, 2–1, though I wasn't involved in the game. At Wembley, Charlie scored both goals, but because he was a bit of a player in the nightclubs, George didn't want him around. Three games into the 1987–88 season he was dropped and never played again. George later sold him. I was gutted when I heard the news, because he was such a top bloke to be around. I never saw him turn up for training with the hump. Even when things weren't going well, or the goals weren't going in, he always had a smile on his face.

He wasn't the only one to be shown the door. George could see a lot of the lads were going out on the town, and they weren't winning anything big, so he decided to make some serious changes. During the 1987–88 season players like David 'Rocky' Rocastle, Michael 'Mickey' Thomas, Tony Adams and Martin Hayes started to make the first team regularly. I was getting a lot of games too, featuring 17 times and scoring five goals, though over half those appearances came as sub.

Looking back, it was obvious what George was doing. He wanted to be around young players who could be bossed about. He wanted to put his authority on the team. Seasoned pros like Charlie wouldn't have fallen in line with his ideas, not in the same way as a bunch of wet-behind-the-ears kids.

Full-backs Nigel Winterburn of Wimbledon and Stoke's Lee Dixon joined the club and were followed in June 1988 by centre-half Steve Bould. Apparently, Lee had been at about 30 clubs, but I'd never heard of him before. The team transformation didn't end with the defence. He also signed striker Alan 'Smudger' Smith from Leicester City. All of a sudden we were a really exciting, young side and everyone was thinking, 'Bloody hell, this could work.'

We only finished sixth in the League in 1987-88, but the new Arsenal were starting to glue. Rocky, God bless him, was one of the best wingers of his generation. He had everything. He could pass the ball, score goals and take people on. But he was also hard as nails and could really put in a tackle. At the same time he was one of the nicest blokes ever and nobody ever said a bad word about him, which in football was a massive compliment. What a player – he should have played a million times for England and he was Arsenal through and through. When George sold him to Leeds in 1992, he was devastated, it broke his heart. It broke our hearts when he died of cancer in 2001.

We used to call Mickey Thomas 'Pebbles', after the gargling baby in *The Flintstones*, because you could never understand what he was saying, he always mumbled, but he was an unbelievable player. When it came to training, George rarely let us have five-a-side games, maybe on a Friday if we were lucky. When we did play them, he always sent Mickey inside to get changed. Because he was such a good footballer, Mickey would always take the piss out of the rest of us, and George wasn't having that. Everything had to be done seriously, or there was no point in doing it at all.

Centre-half Steve Bould was the best addition to the first-team squad as far as I was concerned, because along with midfielder Perry Groves, who was signed from Colchester in 1986, he became one of my drinking partners at the club. His main talent, apart from being a professional footballer, was eating. Bloody hell, he could put it away. On the way home from away games, there was always a fancy table service on the coach, complete with two waiters. The squad would have a prawn cocktail to start, or maybe some salmon or a soup. Then there was a choice of a roast dinner or pasta for the main course, with an apple pie as dessert. That was followed up with cheese and biscuits. In the meantime, the team would get stuck into the lagers. If we'd won, I'd always grab a couple of crates from the players' lounge on the way out.

Bouldy was six foot four and I swear he was hollow. We'd have eating competitions to kill time on the journey and he would win every time. Prawn cocktails, soup, salmon, roast chicken, lasagnes, apple pies, cheese and biscuits – he'd eat the whole menu and then some. Everything was washed down with can after can of lager. By the time the coach pulled into the training ground car park, we'd fall off it. I'd have to call my missus for a lift because I couldn't drive home, but Bouldy always seemed as fresh as a daisy as he made the journey back to his gaff. He probably stopped for a curry on the way.

George worked us hard, really hard, and training was a nightmare. On Monday, we'd run in the countryside. On Tuesday, we'd run all morning at Highbury until we were sick. We'd do old-school exercises, like sprinting up and down the terraces and giving piggybacks along the North Bank. Modern-day players wouldn't stand for it, they'd be crying to their agents every day, but George could get away with it because we were young and keen and not earning huge amounts of money. We didn't have any power.

Still, it was like Groundhog Day and I could have told you, to the drill, what I was doing every single day of the week for the first three months of the 1988-89 season. Most of it was based on the defensive side of the game, George was obsessed by it. We would carry out drills where two teams had to keep possession for as long as possible, then we'd work with eight players keeping the ball against two runners.

In another session, George would set up a back six of John Lukic in goal, Lee Dixon and Nigel Winterburn as full-backs, and Tony and Bouldy as centre-halves, with David O'Leary protecting them in the midfield. A team of 11 players would then try to break them down. They were phenomenal defensively. If we scored more than one goal against them in training, we knew we'd done well. Sometimes George would link the back four with a rope, so when they ran out to catch a striker offside, they would get used to coming out together, arms in the air, shouting at the lino. It wasn't a fluke that clean sheets were common for us in those days, because George worked so hard to achieve them.

We did the same thing every day, but the lads never moaned. If anyone grumbled they were soon dropped for the next match, and so we worked every morning on not conceding goals without a murmur. Everyone listened to George, because we were all frightened of what he would do if we didn't live up to his high standards. He was nothing like the laid-back player everyone had heard about.

Do Not Drink 15 Pints and Crash Your Car ...

As a tactician he was brilliant, and his knowledge was scary, but he was even scarier as a bloke. If you didn't do what he'd said, like getting the ball beyond the first man at a corner, he'd bollock you badly. When George walked into a room, everybody stopped talking, and nobody ever dared to challenge him if they thought what he was doing was wrong or out of order.

Our defender (or defensive midfielder, depending on the line-up) Martin Keown was the only person to have a go at George in all the time I was there. I remember we went to Ipswich and had a nightmare. God knows why the argument started, but it ended up with Martin shouting at George in the dressing-room – giving it, trying to start a ruck.

'Come on, George!' he yelled as the lads stared, open-mouthed. 'Come on!' He didn't play for ages after that.

Fans wondered why George didn't stay around the game much longer than he did, but it's pretty obvious really – the players wouldn't stand for his methods of management today. They earn too much money, they wouldn't have to listen to him. They'd be moaning in the papers and asking for a move as soon as he'd got them giving piggybacks in training.

How Not To Be a Professional Footballer

Wednesdays were great because George always gave the squad a day off. That meant I could get hammered on a Tuesday night, which I did every week. Often I was joined by some of the other lads, like Steve Bould, Tony Adams, Nigel Winterburn and Perry Groves. We'd start off in a local pub, then we'd go into London and drink all over town. We wouldn't stop until we were paro. The pint-o-meter usually came in at 15 beers plus and we used to call our sessions 'The Tuesday Club'. George knew about the heavy nights, but I don't think he cared because we were always right as rain when we arrived for training on Thursday.

Bouldy was always up for a drink in those days, as was Grovesy, but he was a bit lighter than the rest of us. Sometimes he'd even throw his lagers away if he thought we weren't looking. I remember the night of Grovesy's first Tuesday Club meeting. It took place during his first week at the club, and we went to a boozer near Highbury. He stood by a big plant as we started sinking the pints, and when we weren't looking he'd tip his drink into the pot. Grovesy threw away so much beer that by the end of the evening the plant was trying to kiss him. When we went back to training on Thursday, everyone was going on about what a big drinker he was, because he'd been the last man standing.

The following week we went into the same pub and one of the lads stood next to the plant. I think they'd worked out that Grovesy wasn't the big hitter we'd thought he'd been, and he was right. After three drinks, Grovesey was paro and couldn't walk. As he staggered around the pub an hour later, he confessed that he'd been chucking his drinks because he was a lightweight. That tag didn't last long, though. After one season, he'd learnt how to keep up with the rest of us. He joined Arsenal a teetotaller and left a serious drinker.

It wasn't just Tuesday nights that we'd go for it – I'd take any excuse for a piss-up. My problem came from the fact that I used booze to put my head right, to calm me down or perk me up. When I was a YTS player, drinking stopped the panic attacks, but when I started breaking into the first team, beer maintained the excitement of playing in front of thousands of Arsenal fans.

It's a massive buzz playing football, especially when everything is new, like when I got my first touches against Man City at Highbury, or that goal at Plough Lane. The adrenaline that came with playing on a Saturday gave me such a rush. And if I scored, it was the best feeling in the world, nothing else came close. The problems started when I realised the buzz was short. I felt flat when I left the pitch, and I'd sit in the dressing-room after a game, thinking, 'What am I going to do now? I can't wait until next Saturday.' And that's where the drinking came in. It kept my high up.

I should have known better, because before I'd made it into the first team regularly, boozing had already got me into trouble. When I was 18, I got done for drink-driving. It was in the summer of 1986, I went to a place called Wheathampstead with a few people and we rounded the night off in the Rose and Crown, a lovely little boozer near my house. After a lorryload of pints, I decided to drive home, pissed out of my face, though I must have crashed into every other car outside the pub as I reversed from my parking spot. I missed the turning for my house, went into the next road and ploughed into a lamppost, which ended up in someone's garden.

I panicked. I ran back to the Rose and Crown and sat there with my mates like nothing had happened. My plan was to pretend that the car had been stolen. It wasn't long before the police arrived and a copper was tapping me on the back.

'Excuse me, Mr Merson,' he said. 'Do you know your car has been crashed into a lamppost which is now in someone's garden?'

I played dumb. 'You're kidding?'

'Has it been stolen?' he asked.

I kept cool. It wasn't hard, I'd been taking plenty of fluids. 'Well, it must have been,' I said, 'because I've been here all night.'

The copper seemed to believe me. He offered to take me to the car, which I knew was in a right state, but just as I was leaving the pub a little old lady shouted out to us. She'd been sat there for ages, watching me.

'He's just got in here!' she shouted. 'He tried to drive his car home!'

That was it, I was done for and the policeman breathalysed me. In the cells an officer told me I'd been three times over the limit.

'Shit, is that bad?' I said.

He shrugged. 'Yeah,' he said. 'But it's not the worst one we've had tonight. We've just pulled a guy for being six times over. But he was driving a JCB through St Albans town centre.'

I was banned from driving for 18 months; the club suspended me for two weeks and fined me £350. Like that JCB in St Albans town centre, I was spinning out of control.

George said the same thing to me whenever I got into trouble: 'Remember who you are. Remember what you are. And remember who you represent.'

That never dropped with me, I never got it. I was just a normal lad. I came from a council estate. My dad was a coal man. My mum worked in a Hoover factory at Hangar Lane. We were normal people and I wanted to live my life as normally as I could. I had the best job in the world, but I still wanted to have a pint with my mates. Along the way, that attitude was my downfall.

The club never really cottoned on that the drinking was starting to become a problem for me. They would

never have believed that I was on my way to being a serious alcoholic. I didn't know either. I thought I was a big
hitter in the boozing department and that it was all under
control. The first I knew of my alcohol problem was when
they told me in the Marchwood rehab centre.

I used to put on weight because of the beer, but the
Arsenal coaches never sussed. I'd worked out that when
I stood on the club weights and the doc took his meas-
urements, I could literally hold the weight off if I lent at
the right angle or nudged the scales in the right way. The
lads used to give me grief all the time. They used to point
at my love handles and say I was pregnant, and when
George walked past me in the dressing-room I'd suck
my tummy in to hide the bulge. I could never have
worn the silly skin-tight shirts they wear now, my gut
was that bad.

People outside the club would see me drinking, and
George would get letters of complaint, but I used to brush
them aside when he read them out to me.

'Paul Merson was in so and so bar in Islington,' he'd
read, sitting behind his desk, waving the letters around.
'He was drunk and a disgrace to Arsenal Football Club.'

I'd make out they were from Tottenham fans. Then,
when I got a letter banging on about how I'd been spotted
drunk in town when I'd really been away with the club on
a winter break, I was made up. I knew from then on I had
proof that there were liars making stuff up about me. I

blamed them for every letter to the club after that, even though most of them were telling the truth.

I wasn't the only one causing aggro, my team-mates were having a right old go, too. In 1989, the year we won the title, I bought a fancy, new, one-bedroom house in Sandridge, near St Albans. It was lovely, fitted with brand-new furniture. I loved it, I was proud of my new home.

Tony Adams was one of my first guests, but he outstayed his welcome. In April 1989 we played Man United away, drew 1–1 and Tone got two goals, one for us and a blinding own goal for them. He fancied a drink afterwards, like he always did in those days, but time was running out as the coach crawled back to London at a snail's pace and we knew the pubs would be kicking out soon. That wasn't going to stop him, though.

'We're not going to get back till nearly 11, Merse,' he said. 'Can I stay at yours and we'll have a few?'

I was up for it. I never needed an excuse for a drink, but at that stage in the campaign, we'd been under a hell of a lot of pressure. We'd started the season on fire, and even though we weren't a worldy side (nowhere near as good as the team that won the title in 1991), at one stage we were top of the First Division by 15 points. Then it all went pear. We'd drawn too many matches against the likes of QPR, Millwall and Charlton. Shaky defeats at Forest and

How Not To Be a Professional Footballer

Coventry had put massive dents in our championship hopes. After leading the title race for the first half of the season our form had dropped big-time and Liverpool were hot on our heels. That night I wanted to let off steam.

I knew I could get a lock-in at the Rose and Crown. I called up my missus and asked her to make up our fancy brand-new sofa bed for Tone when we got back. Once the team coach pulled up at the training ground, we got into Tone's car and drove to the pub.

We finished our last pint at four in the morning. Tone gave me a lift back to the house and nearly killed us twice, before parking in the street at some stupid angle. I crept inside, not wanting to wake Lorraine, put Tone to bed and crashed out. When I woke up later, Lorraine was standing over me with a copy of the *Daily Mirror* in her hand.

'Look at what they've done to him!' she said, showing me the back page.

Some smart-arse editor had drawn comedy donkey ears on a photo of Tone. Underneath was the headline, 'Eeyore Adams'. And all because he'd scored an own goal. He'd got one for us too, but that didn't seem to matter.

'What a nightmare,' I said.

'Are you going to tell him?'

'Bollocks am I, let him find out when he's filling up at the petrol station.'

Do Not Drink 15 Pints and Crash Your Car...

I could hear Tone getting his stuff together downstairs. Then he shouted out to us, 'See you later, Merse! Thanks for letting me stay, Lorraine!'

When I heard the front door go, I knew we were off the hook. Lorraine got up to sort the sofa bed out so we could watch the telly, and I got up to make a cup of tea. Then Lorraine started shouting. 'He's pissed the bed!'

I looked over to see her pointing at a wet patch on our brand-new furniture. I was furious. I grabbed the paper and chased down the street after Tone as he pulled away in his car.

'You donkey, Adams!' I shouted. 'You're a fucking donkey!'

LESSON 3

Do Not Cross Gorgeous George

'Because hell hath no fury like a gaffer scorned.'

After Tone's bed-wetting incident and the 1-1 draw with Man United, Arsenal started to fly again. We beat Everton, Newcastle and Boro and spanked Norwich 5-0. The only moody result was a 2-1 away defeat at Derby County which allowed Liverpool to leapfrog us in the League with one game to go. Along the way, I got us some important goals. There was an equaliser in a 2-2 draw against Wimbledon in the last home game of the season which kept us in the chase for the League, but my favourite was a strike against Everton in the 3-1 win at Goodison Park. I got on to the end of a long ball over the top and banged it home. When it flew past their keeper, Neville Southall, I ran up to the Arsenal fans, hanging on to the cage that separated the terraces from the pitch.

I loved celebrating with the Arsenal crowd. It was a completely different atmosphere at football matches back then. There was a real edge to the games. Remember, this was a time before the Hillsborough disaster and the Taylor Report and there were hardly any seats in football grounds. Well, not when you compare them with today's fancy stadiums. The fans swayed about and the grounds had an unbelievable atmosphere. I loved it when there were terraces. Football hooliganism was a real problem back then, though. It could get a bit naughty sometimes.

I'd always learn through mates and fans when there was going to be trouble in the ground. If Arsenal were playing Chelsea at Highbury, I'd always hear whispers that their lot would be planning on taking the North Bank in a mass ruck. The players would talk about it in the dressing-room before games, and whenever there was a throw-in or a break in the play, I'd look up at the stands, just to see if it was kicking off.

You could have a bit of fun with the supporters in those days, and we often laughed and joked with them during the games. If ever we were playing away and the home lot were hurling insults at us, we'd give it back when the ref wasn't looking. It happened off the pitch as well, but sometimes we went too far.

How Not To Be a Professional Footballer

I remember when Arsenal played Chelsea at Stamford Bridge in 1993. After the game a group of their fans started chucking abuse at our team bus, they were even banging on the windows. I was sat at the back, waiting for Steve Bould's eating competition to kick off, when all of a sudden our striker, Ian Wright, started to make wanker signs over the top of the seats. All the fans could see was his hand through the back window, waving away. They couldn't believe it.

I nearly pissed myself laughing as the coach pulled off, but I wasn't so happy when we suddenly stopped a hundred yards down the road. The traffic lights had turned red and Chelsea's mob were right on top of the bus. They were throwing stuff at the windows, lobbing bottles and stones towards Wrighty's seat. All I could think was, 'Oh God, please don't let them get on, they'll kill us.' Luckily the lights changed quickly enough for us to pull away unhurt. I don't think anyone had a pop at the fans for quite a while after that.

All of a sudden, I was in the big time and so were Arsenal. By the time the 1988-89 season was in full swing, my name was everywhere and I had a big reputation. George had made me a regular in his team and I'd started 35 games, scoring 14 times as centre-forward. I did so well I was awarded the PFA Young Player of the Year. I even had nicknames – the Highbury crowd called me 'Merse' or 'The Magic Man'. There was probably some less flattering stuff as well, but I didn't pay any attention to that.

With our defeat at Derby and draw against Wimbledon, and Liverpool's 5-1 win over West Ham, the title boiled down to the last game of the season, an away game at Anfield on Friday 26 May. Liverpool were top of the table by three points, we were second. Fair play to them, they'd been brilliant all year and hadn't lost a game since 1 January. We still had a chance, though. We knew that if we did them by two goals at Anfield, we'd pinch it on goal difference.

Anfield was the ultimate place to play as a footballer back then. Before a Saturday game at Liverpool, probably around 1.30, the away team would go on to the pitch to have a walk around. George liked us to check out the surface and soak up the atmosphere on away days. Anfield was always buzzing because the Kop was packed from lunchtime. They'd sing 'You'll Never Walk Alone', wave their scarves, and surge backwards and forwards, side to side, like they were all on a nightmare ferry crossing to France. It always made me double nervous.

'Oh shit,' I'd think. 'Here we go.'

Weirdly, I wasn't nervous when we played them at their place on the last day of the 1988–89 season, mainly because nobody had given us a cat-in-hell's chance of winning the League. Nobody won by two goals at Anfield in those days. Before the game, my attitude was, 'No way, mate. It ain't happening.'

The game had become a title decider because of the Hillsborough disaster. It had originally been scheduled for April, but after the FA Cup semi-final between Liverpool and Forest at Sheffield Wednesday's ground, where 96 Liverpool fans were crushed to death in the stands before kick-off, it was postponed until the end of May, after the final. Liverpool got through against Forest and won the FA Cup, beating Everton of all teams 3–2, not that any Everton fan would begrudge them after all that. Now it was up to us to stop them from doing the double.

I could understand the faffing about with the fixtures, because Hillsborough was one of the worst things I'd ever seen in football. In 1985, I'd watched the Heysel Stadium disaster on the telly. It made me feel sick. I'd turned on the telly hoping to see the European Cup Final between Liverpool and Juventus, but instead I watched as bodies were being carried out. A riot had kicked off, and as fans tried to escape the trouble a wall collapsed on them. Hillsborough was just as bad. I was supposed to pick up my PFA Young Player of the Year Award at a fancy ceremony on the day that it happened, but after seeing the tragedy on the news, I really wasn't interested. Everything seemed insignificant after all those deaths.

The fixture change pushed us together on the last day of the season in a grand finale. Because the odds were

Do Not Cross Gorgeous George

stacked against us and everyone was writing Arsenal off, it had become a free game for the lads, a bonus ball on the calendar. In our heads, we knew George had turned the team around after Don had resigned. Considering Arsenal hadn't won the League for ages, coming second in the old First Division in 1989 would have been considered a massive achievement by everyone, even though we'd been top for ages before falling away. We were still a young side, discovering our potential, and there was no shame in being runners-up behind an awesome Liverpool team that included legends like Ian Rush, John Aldridge, John Barnes, Peter Beardsley and Steve McMahon. It would have been phenomenal really.

George still pumped us full of confidence. During the week before the game he banged on about how good we were and how we could beat Liverpool. He planned everything as meticulously as he planned his appearance, which was always immaculate. We went up to Merseyside on the morning of the game that Friday, because George wanted to cut out the nerves that would have built up overnight if the team had stayed together. We got into our hotel in Liverpool's town centre at midday, ate lunch together and then went to our rooms for a three-hour kip.

I never roomed with anyone in those days, because nobody would share with me. The main reason was that I could never get to sleep. I was too excitable and that always drove the other lads mad. Nobody wanted to deal with my messing around before a big game, but in the end I got to enjoy my own privacy. The great thing about having a room to myself was that I could wax the dolphin whenever I wanted.

At five-thirty we all went downstairs for the tactical meeting and some tea and toast. George lifted up a white board and named the team: John Lukic in goal; a back five of Lee Dixon, Nigel Winterburn, Tone and Bouldy, with David O'Leary acting as a sweeper. All very continental. I was in midfield with Rocky, Mickey and Kevin Richardson. Alan Smith was playing up front on his own. George told us who was picking up who at set-pieces, and then he told us how to win the game.

'Listen, don't go out there and try to score two goals in the first 20 minutes,' he said. 'Keep it tight in the first half, because if they score first, we'll have to get three or four goals at Anfield and that's next to impossible. Get in at half-time with the game nil-nil.

'In the second half, you'll go out and score. Then, with 15 minutes to go, I'll change the team around, they'll shit themselves, you'll have a right old go, score again and win the game 2–0. OK?'

Everyone looked at each other with their jaws open. Remember, Liverpool hadn't lost since New Year's Day. I turned round to Bouldy and said, 'Is he on what I'm on here?'

None of us believed it was going to happen, not in a million years, but we really should have had more faith in

Do Not Cross Gorgeous George

George. He was one of those managers who had so much football knowledge it was scary. People said he was lucky during his career, but George made his own luck. Things happened for him because he worked for it. He was always saying stuff like, 'Fail to prepare, prepare to fail.' He'd read big books like *The Art of War*. I couldn't understand any of it.

When we kicked off, I thought George had lost the plot. In the first half, Liverpool passed us to death. I touched the ball twice and we never looked like scoring. They never looked like scoring either, but they didn't have to. A 0-0 draw would have won them the title, so they were probably made up at half-time. The really weird thing was, George was made up as well.

'Great stuff, lads,' he said. 'Brilliant, perfect. Absolutely outstanding. The plan's going perfectly.'

I couldn't make it out. George was never happy at half-time. We could have been beating Barcelona 100-0 and he'd still be angry about something. I turned round to Mickey.

'You touched it yet?' I said.

He shrugged his shoulders. Everyone was looking at the gaffer in disbelief.

Then we went out and scored, just like George had reckoned we would. It came from a free-kick. The ball was whipped in and Alan Smith claimed he got his head to it. I wasn't sure whether it had come off his nose, but I couldn't have cared less – we were 1–0 up. It could have been even better, because moments later Mickey was bearing down on Bruce Grobbelaar's goal, one-on-one. In those days, you had to have some neck to win 2–0 at Anfield. Often the Kop would virtually blow the ball out of the net. It must have freaked Mickey out because he fluffed it. All I could think was, 'Shit, we've blown the League.'

Then it was game over, well, for me anyway. George took me off and brought on winger Martin Hayes, pushing him up front. Then he pulled off Bouldy and switched to 4-4-2 by replacing him with Grovesy, an extra midfielder. This was where Liverpool were supposed to shit themselves, but I was the one who was terrified. I had to watch the closing minutes like every other fan.

We were playing injury time. Their England midfielder, Steve McMahon was running around, wagging his finger and telling the Liverpool lot we only had a minute left to play. Winger John Barnes won the ball down by the corner flag in our half. He was one of the best English players I'd ever seen, but God knows what he was doing that night. All he had to do was hang on to possession and run down the clock, but for some reason he tried to cut inside his man. Nigel Winterburn nicked the ball off him and rolled it back to John Lukic who gave it a big lump down field. There was a flick on, and suddenly Mickey was one-on-one with Grobbelaar again.

Do Not Cross Gorgeous George

This time, he dinked the ball over him. It was one of the best goals I'd ever seen, one of those chips the South Americans call 'The Falling Leaf' – where a player pops the ball over an advancing keeper. It was never going to be easy for Mickey to chip someone like Grobbelaar, especially after missing a sitter earlier in the game, and he had a thousand years to think about what he was going to do as he pelted towards goal – talk about pressure. Mickey kept his head and his goal snatched a famous 2–0 victory and the League title.

When I think about it, that's probably one of the most famous games ever. Even if you supported someone like Halifax, Rochdale or Aldershot at that time, you'd still remember that match, especially the moment when commentator Brian Moore screamed, 'It's up for grabs now!' on the telly, or the image of Steve McMahon wagging his finger, giving it the big one. Afterwards he was sat on his arse. He looked gutted.

It was extra special for Arsenal. We hadn't won the League for 18 years and the Kop later applauded us off the pitch. It was a nice touch. Liverpool were the best team in the land at that time. They probably figured another title would turn up at their place, sooner rather than later.

The celebrations started straight after the game. I cracked open a bottle of beer with Bouldy in the dressing-room, still in my muddy Arsenal kit. After that, we got paro on the coach home and ended up in a Cockfosters nightclub until silly o'clock. There was an open-topped bus parade on the Sunday, but everything is a blur to me. The next thing I remember it was breakfast time on Tuesday morning. I was trying to get my keys into my front door, waking up the whole street. I still haven't got a clue what happened in those 72 hours or so in between. These days, whenever a 22-year-old comes up to me and asks for an autograph, the same thought flashes through my mind: 'Oh, for fuck's sake, please don't call me Dad.'

The lads at the club called me 'Son of George' because they reckoned I got away with murder. They were probably right. I certainly didn't get bollocked as much by the manager as the others, even though I was probably the most badly behaved player in the squad. For some reason, George really took a shine to me.

I remember one time when we went to a summer tournament in Miami in 1990. It was a bloody nightmare. The weather was so hot we had to train at 8.30 in the morning. One day, I stood on the sidelines, yawning, scratching my cods, when George jogged over and looked at my hand. It was halfway down my shorts.

'You all right, Merse?'

'Yeah, I'm fine,' I said.

George put his arm around my shoulder. 'No, no, you sit down, son,' he said, thinking I'd pulled a groin muscle.

Do Not Cross Gorgeous George

He was worried I might have overdone it in training, but the only thing I'd been overdoing was a little dolphin waxing in my hotel room.

'Sit out this session, and don't worry about it,' he said.

I could see what the rest of the lads were thinking as I lazed around on the sidelines, and it wasn't complimentary. Moments later, Grovesy and Bouldy started rubbing their own wedding tackles, groaning, hoping they'd get some of the same treatment, but George was having none of it.

That was how it was with me and George, he was good as gold all the time. He always told me up-front when I wasn't playing, whether that was because he was dropping me or resting me. He knew I couldn't physically cope with playing five games on the bounce because I'd be knackered. He liked to rest me every now and then, but he always gave me a heads-up. With the other lads, George wouldn't announce the news until he'd named the team in the Friday tactical meeting. It would come as a shock to them and that was always a nightmare, because the whole squad would make noises and pull faces. George would always pull me to one side on Thursday, so I could tell the lads myself, as if I'd made the decision. He'd never let me roast.

As I went more and more off the rails throughout my Arsenal career, he must have given me a million chances.

How Not To Be a Professional Footballer

God knows why. After my run-ins with the law and the drink-driving charge, word got around the club about my problems, and George started to get fed up with the drinking stories as they started to happen more regularly. I was forever in his office for a lecture. If I'd been caught drinking again or misbehaving, he would remind me of my responsibilities, but he'd never threaten to kick me out of the club or sell me, even though I was high maintenance off the pitch.

I was saved by the fact that I never had any problems training. No matter how paro I'd got the night before, I rarely had a hangover the next morning, I was lucky. I could always tell when some players had been drinking by the way they acted in practice games – they couldn't hack it. Me, I could always get up and play. I didn't enjoy it, but I could get through the day, and George knew that come Saturday I'd be as good as gold for him.

Well, most of the time. In some games I played while still pissed from the previous night. In 1991 we faced Luton Town away on Boxing Day. On Christmas Day, the players had their lunches at home with the families, then we met up at Highbury for training. Afterwards, we piled on to the coach to the team hotel and I knocked back pints and pints and pints in the bar. I couldn't help it, it was Christmas and I was in the mood. The next day, I was still hammered. During the game, a long ball came over and I chased after it. As I got within a few yards I tripped over my own feet, even though there wasn't a soul near me. I could hear everyone in the crowd laughing and jeering. I couldn't look towards the bench.

Even though I was Son of George, the manager would always bollock me really hard whenever he caught me drinking. I was even the first player ever to be banned from Arsenal when I caused a lorryload of trouble at an official dinner and dance event for the club at London's Grosvenor House Hotel. The ban was only for two weeks in 1989, but it caused one hell of a stink all the same.

I was hitting the booze pretty hard that night, and this was a fancy do with dinner jackets, a big meal, and loads of beers flying around. I got smashed big-time, drinking at the bar and having a right old laugh. I was so loud that my shouting drowned out the hired comedian, Norman Collier, who was entertaining the club's guests - including wives, directors and VIP big shots. People turned round and stared at me as I knocked back drink after drink. George and the Arsenal board were taking note.

Later, a big punch-up kicked off in the car park outside the hotel and somehow I was in the thick of it. To this day I still don't know what happened, because I was so paro. The papers got to hear about the scuffle, and so did the fans. The next day, George told me to sort myself out and not to come back for a couple of weeks. I wasn't even allowed to train and being shut out scared me.

How Not To Be a Professional Footballer

I spent a fortnight lying low, trying to convince myself that I'd get back on the straight and narrow. For a while it worked. When I came back I was as good as gold, then I started downing the beers again. The Tuesday Club was into the swing of things and I was back on the slippery slope.

I got worse, and whenever I messed up and George found out, he would do me. On New Year's Day in 1990, we were playing Crystal Palace at Selhurst Park. I was told I wasn't in the team.

'Nice one,' I thought. 'It's New Year's Eve and I'm in a fancy hotel with the rest of the team, let's get paro.'

I figured being dropped was a green light for me to go out for a drink and a party. This time, I got so smashed I couldn't even get up in the morning. George found out and named me as sub for the match just to teach me a lesson. When I fell asleep on the bench during the game, he brought me on for the last 10 minutes to give me another slap. I couldn't do a thing – I was like a fish up a tree. I couldn't control the ball and I felt sick every time I sprinted down the wing. We won 4–1, but after that night George vowed never to name a team on New Year's Eve again. On a normal Saturday he would have got away with it, because I'd have behaved, but I was becoming an alcoholic and it was New Year's Eve. It had been a recipe for disaster.

LESSON 4

Do Not Shit on David Seaman's Balcony

'More boozy disasters for our football dynamo; Perry Groves nearly drowns.'

Oh my God, Gus Caesar was as hard as nails. When he played in the Arsenal defence he always had a ricket in his locker and the fans sometimes got on his back a little bit because he made the odd cock-up, but what he lacked in technique he definitely made up for in physique. He was the muscliest footballer I'd ever seen. I reckon he could have killed someone with a Bruce Lee-style one-inch punch if he wanted. A lot of the time, I got the impression he was just waiting for an excuse to try it out on me. I had a habit of rubbing him up the wrong way.

It all kicked off with me and Gus in 1989, when Arsenal took the players away to Bermuda for a team holiday. The whole squad went to a nightclub and got on the beers one night, messing around, having a laugh. All of a sudden Gus started shouting at me. A drunken argument over nothing, a spilt pint maybe, had got out of hand. A scuffle broke out – handbags stuff, really – and Gus poked me in the eye just as the pair of us were being separated.

It bloody hurt and I was proper angry, but because I wasn't much of a fighter I knew that poking Gus back would have been stupid. He would have torn me limb from limb. I reckoned on a better way to get my own back, so I let the commotion calm down, staggering away, bellyaching, checking to see if I was permanently blind. Then Bouldy and me went back to the hotel, leaving everyone behind. We walked up to reception, casual as you like, and blagged the key to Gus's door. It was party time, I was going to cause some serious damage to his room.

In hindsight it was a suicidal move, because Gus was sharing with midfielder Paul Davis, who was hardly a softie. He'd infamously smacked Southampton's midfield hardman, Glenn Cockerill, in the middle of a game in 1988. The blow knocked him out cold and the punch was all over the papers the next day because it had been caught on the telly. Paul was banned for nine games after the FA had viewed the video evidence, which was unheard-of in those days, and Glenn slurped hospital food through a wired jaw for the best part of a fortnight. We all knew not to cross Paul, but that was in the sober light of day. I was well gone and angry that night, so I didn't care.

Once I'd got into Gus and Paul's room, I went mental and trashed it. I stamped on a very expensive-looking watch and smashed the board games that were lying around on the floor. Footballers didn't have PlayStations in those days, Monopoly was the closest thing we had to entertainment without draining the minibar, and we'd done that already. Then I threw a bucket of water up on to the ceiling, leaving it to drip, drip, drip down throughout the night. It was a five-star hotel, but I couldn't give a toss. I threw a bed out of the balcony window, then me and Bouldy laughed all the way back to our room.

I woke up not long afterwards, still pissed. Everything was swimming back to me – the fight, Gus jabbing me in the eye and the red mist coming down. An imaginary crime scene photo of the trashed hotel room slapped me around the face like a wet cod. In my head it looked like it was *CSI: Merse*. I sat up in bed with that horrible morning-after-the-night-before feeling and started moaning, my head in my hands.

'Oh no, what the fuck have I done?' I whispered.

In a panic I got dressed and padded across the corridor, hoping I could tidy up the mess before the lads got back, but it was too late. Paul Davis had pinned a note to the door.

'Gus, the little shits have busted the room up. Just leave it and go to sleep somewhere else. Paul.'

I crawled back to bed, knowing I was done for. Hours later, the phone in our room started ringing. It was George. He was not happy.

'Room 312. Now!' he shouted.

Bouldy got up. I tried to pull myself together, splashing my face with water and hauling on my shorts and flip flops. It was a lovely day outside, the sun was scorching hot and there wasn't a cloud in the sky, but it might as well have been a pissing wet morning in St Albans for all I cared. I felt sick to the pit of my stomach as we made the Walk of Death to Room 312, which I knew was Paul and Gus's room.

When we walked in, I thought I'd arrived in downtown Baghdad. Water dripped from the ceiling. The board games were in pieces and all the plastic parts were scattered over the floor. It turned out they had belonged to the kids of club vice-chairman David Dein. He'd lent them to the squad for the week, believing we'd appreciate the gesture, seeing as we were grown adults. The balcony window was wide open and I could see a bed upended by the pool outside. Then I realised the lads were sitting there in the room, all of them staring at me. Tone, Lee Dixon, Nigel Winterburn, Alan Smith and George. In the corner, Gus was twitching on a chair with his shirt off. His muscles were rippling and his jaw was clenched shut. His breathing sounded funny. Behind him, Paul Davis was massaging his shoulders, glaring at me like I was a murderer. Gus looked like a prize fighter waiting to pummel somebody.

George stood up and started the dressing-down.

'What's all this, Paul?'

'Yeah, I know boss,' I said. 'Me and Gus had a bit of an argument and I came back here and trashed his room.'

He nodded, weighing up the situation. 'Well, why don't you go outside now and sort it out between yourselves?' he said.

What? I started shaking. Gus looked like a caged Rottweiler gagging for his dinner. I'd sobered up sharpish, because I knew I didn't want to fight Gus – he would have killed me. Gus knew it too and was cracking his knuckles, working the muscles in his upper body. Then Paul Davis piped up.

'Yeah, why don't you go outside and sort it out, Merse? Fight him.'

Fuck that. I backed down, apologised, grovelled, and took my punishment. Nobody spoke to me for two months afterwards, and I was chucked out of the players' pool. That was bad news. The players' pool was a cut of the TV money which was shared out among the team from Arsenal's FA Cup and League Cup runs. That added up to a lot of cash in those days. I could earn more money from the players' pool than from my wages and appearances money put together. I was gutted.

How Not To Be a Professional Footballer

It was George's way to keep us in check through our wallets. When I won the League in 1989, my wages were £300 a week, with a £350 bonus for a win and £200 for an appearance. In a good month I could clock up three or four grand. There were never any goal bonuses in those days, because George reckoned they would have made us greedy, but if you look at the old videos now, you can see we all jumped on one another whenever we scored. That was because we were getting more dough for a win than our weekly wage. Everyone was playing for one another, it was phenomenal, but if you looked at the subs' bench, it was always moody. Life on the sidelines was financially tough for a player, because we were only getting the basic £300.

Still, George made a point of keeping the lads close financially. Some of the team now feel a bit fed up with him because they didn't earn the money they might have done at another big club, and it's true that we were very poorly paid compared to the other teams. But the thing is, all of those players went on to make a lorryload of appearances throughout their careers thanks to him. They earned quite a bit in the long run, so they shouldn't have a bad word to say about the bloke.

It's a million miles away from the game today, but I've got no qualms about top, top players making great money. They're entertainers. Arnold Schwarzenegger makes loads of films and he can't act, but no one says anything about him making £7 million a movie, do they? If a top player gets £100,000 a week in football, the fans say he's earning too much, but players like that are the difference between people going to work on a Monday happy or moody.

Your Steven Gerrards, your Wayne Rooneys – these are the players that should get the serious money. My problem is with the average players getting lorryloads of cash for sitting on the bench. That's where it's wrong. From an early age, players should be paid on appearances, just like George had set us up at Arsenal. They should get 33.3 per cent in wages, 33.3 per cent in appearance money and 33.3 per cent in win bonuses.

It gives the players incentives; it stops people slacking off. I've seen it with certain strikers enough times. They are on fire, then they sign a new contract and never kick the ball again. They don't look interested. They move to a new club and do the same. Those things sicken me, but not all footballers are like that. When you look at players like Ryan Giggs and Paul Scholes, they seem like proper professionals. They score at least eight out of 10 ratings for their performance levels every year, and they've won everything in the game 10 times over. They're still churning it out. I never hear them complaining about money. Well, they're at United, so they probably don't have to.

How Not To Be a Professional Footballer

My mucking around in Bermuda was par for the course really. Every year George liked to take the squad to Marbella in Spain for a short holiday. We'd go three times a season, the idea being that a few days in the sun would freshen the lads up before a big run of games. We'd meet at the airport on a Sunday morning, and by Sunday evening I'd be paro, usually with Grovesy. I loved it.

One year we went away when it was Grovesy's birthday. Neither of us was playing because of injuries, so we went out on the piss, hitting the bars on Marbella's waterfront. By the time we'd staggered into Sinatra's, a pub by the port, all the lads were drinking and getting stuck into dinner. I was hammered. When the condiments came over, I squirted Grovesy with a sachet of tomato ketchup. The sauce splattered his face and fancy white shirt. Grovesy squirted me back with mustard and within seconds we were both smothered in red and yellow mess.

Then the lads joined in. Because it was Grovesy's birthday, we jumped on him and grabbed his arms and legs. Some bright spark suggested dunking him in the sea, which was just over the road. Tourists stared and pointed. God knows what they must have thought as they watched a group of blokes they'd probably recognised from *Match of the Day* staggering across the street, dragging a screaming team-mate towards the tide.

We lobbed him over a small wall and I waited for the splash and Grovesy's screams.

Do Not Shit on David Seaman's Balcony

There was no noise. We couldn't see over the rocks. I started to brick myself. How far down was the water? Nobody had checked before throwing him in.

Finally ... splash!

Then there was screaming – thank God. The lads started laughing, nervously. We peered over the edge and saw a ginger head and thrashing arms. He was about 20 miles below us, thrashing about in the waves. Grovesy was panicking, trying to swim towards the rocks. He was chucking all sorts of abuse at us, so nobody tried to help him out, and nobody offered any sympathy as he squelched all the way home.

Grovesy was used to stick. My party piece was to shit in his pillow case just to really wind him up. I used to love seeing the look on his face as he realised I'd left him a little bedtime pressie. When he caught me the first time, squatting above his bed, letting one go, he couldn't believe his eyes.

'Merse, what the fuck are you doing?' he screamed.

I didn't stop to explain.

When Grovesy left Arsenal for Southampton I was sad to see him go, but when I started sharing a room with midfielder Ray Parlour, I realised I'd found someone who was just as lively. That holiday, George had put us into a room next door to our keeper, David 'Spunky' Seaman, who had signed in 1990, and Lee Dixon. We called them the Straight Batters, because they never got involved with the drinking and messing around like some of us did. They were always the first to bed whenever we went out on the town. I was the complete opposite. I rarely slept on club holidays, and I'd always pay the bar staff a fair few quid to leave out a bin of beers and ice for when we got back from the pub. That way we could drink all night.

One morning Dixon and Spunky went off for a walk while Ray and me snored away our hangovers. When I woke up I needed the khazi, so, still half cut, I thought it would be funny to bunk over the adjoining balcony and put a big shit in front of the Straight Batters' sea view. I didn't think anything of it until a few hours later when I was sitting by the pool with Ray, soaking up the sun. Suddenly I could hear Spunky going ballistic. His deep, northern voice was booming around the hotel and scaring the seagulls away.

'Ooh the fook's done that?!' he yelled.

Me and Ray were falling about by the pool. Like he needed to ask.

Even though Arsenal didn't retain the title in 1990, we were a team on the up. Liverpool ran away with it that year and I soon learnt that everyone wanted to beat the champions, which made the games so much harder than before. We got spanked 4-1 by Man U away on the first day of the season. It was a real eye-opening experience. I remember that game well, not just because of the battering we took, but because United's supposed next chairman, Michael Knighton, came out on to the pitch making a big song and dance, showing off about how he was going to buy the club. He had his United shirt on and he came out doing all these keepy-ups, while we stared at him.

'Who the fuck is this bloke?' I thought.

He smashed the ball home and waved to the crowd as he ran off. It turned out that he didn't have quite the financial backing the fans thought he had.

The United game set the tone for the season, and we lost too many important games during the campaign – Liverpool, Spurs, Southampton, Wimbledon, Sheffield Wednesday, QPR and Chelsea all managed to beat us along the way. It was hardly the form of champions. We ended up in fourth spot, which was disappointing after the year before.

The fact that we weren't going to win the League that year caused complacency to creep in among some of the lads, and George hated that. On the last day of the season we were due to play Norwich City. Liverpool were streets ahead. We couldn't qualify for Europe because of the ban on English teams after the Heysel disaster, and we couldn't go down, so it was a nothing game really.

I was injured, and the day before the match was a scorcher. I got together with Bouldy, Grovesy and Nigel, and after training we strolled down to a nearby tennis club for a pint. We had three beers each and some of the other lads came in at different times and had a beer or two and left, but the bar staff didn't collect the bottles as we sat there. After an hour the table was swamped with empties. Then George walked in with his coaching staff, jumper draped over his shoulders like Prince Charles on a summer stroll.

The thing with Gorgeous George was that he was proud of his looks and he liked to live in luxury. One time, when we flew economy to Australia for a six-a-side tournament with Man City and Forest, George sat in first class while the great Brian Clough sat in the same seats as the players. The message was clear: George wanted to keep his distance.

Now he eyed the bottles.

'Having a good time, lads?' he said, happy as you like.

'Yeah, cheers, boss,' we said, thinking we'd got away with it.

As he strolled off, I honestly thought that was the end of the matter. In fact, he didn't mention it again all weekend. As far as we were concerned it was forgotten. We drew 2–2 with Norwich, and the following day we flew to Singapore for seven days to play Liverpool in an exhibition match before showing up in a few friendlies with local sides. It was all Mickey Mouse stuff, really. The plan was to stay there for a week because the club were treating the players to another seven days in Bali for a holiday and we were flying out of Singapore.

I couldn't wait, I was like a kid on Christmas Eve. The morning of our Bali flight, I sat in the hotel foyer at 10 in the morning with my bags packed. Bouldy, Grovesy and Nigel were also with me when George walked up. In those days, the clubs held on to the player's passports, probably to stop us from doing a runner to Juventus or Lazio for bigger money, but George had ours in his hands.

'Right, lads,' he said, handing them out one by one. 'Your flight home to London leaves in three hours. I'll see you when we get back from our holiday.'

There was a stunned silence as George turned his back on us to take the rest of the lads to Bali for a jolly. We were later told it was because we'd been caught drinking before the Norwich game. Our summer hols had been cancelled, but I don't think my case had been helped when I was caught throwing an ashtray at a punter in a Singapore nightclub a few nights earlier. We were later fined two-weeks' wages. On the way home nobody spoke, we didn't even drink on the plane. I only used to have a beer when I knew I wasn't supposed to have one. That day it hardly seemed worth it.

I should have guessed that George would let loose on the Singapore trip, because in between the beers at Norwich and our early flight home, Tone had been done for drink-driving. As a defender, he was top, top drawer and would run through a brick wall for Arsenal. The problem was, he'd driven through one as well, pissed out of his face the night before we were due to fly east. The police turned up and gave him the breathalyser test, and Tone was nicked. He was the Arsenal captain and well over the limit. Someone was always going to cop it from the gaffer after that.

The funny thing was, when Tone turned up late at the airport looking like he'd been dragged through a hedge, nobody said anything at first. We'd been waiting for him at the airport for so long that it looked like he wasn't going to show. We were just relieved to be getting on the plane. It was only when he got into his seat and said, 'Bloody hell, I've been done for drink-driving,' that we got an idea of what had happened, but even then nobody batted an eyelid because we all knew he was a Billy Bullshitter.

Tone was forever making stuff up, and he'd built up quite a reputation around the club. I could be sitting there at the training ground, reading the *Sun*, and just as I was turning over to Page 3 for an eyeful, he'd lean across.

'I've fucked her,' he'd say, pointing to the girl in the picture.

'Piss off, Tone,' I used to say. 'You look like Jimmy Nail.'

Then he ended up going out with Caprice for a while. She was a model, and a right fit one at that, so maybe he was getting lucky with Britain's favourite lovelies after all. That day, though, no one was having it. Even as he was brushing glass from his hair on the plane, the lads thought he was pulling a fast one.

When we got to Singapore we knew it wasn't a wind-up because it was all over the news. By the time the English papers had turned up, the whole club knew about it. Everyone at home was making out he was a disgrace to football, and the fans were worried that he might buckle under the pressure, but Tone had a seriously strong character. If anyone was going to get through it unscathed it was him.

You have to remember that he'd already shouldered a lot of pressure. When he made his Arsenal debut against Sunderland in 1983 he'd been ripped to shreds by a striker called Colin West. Tone was only 17 and it was probably one of the worst debuts by a defender in the history of the game. The golden rule of football is that everyone has a good debut – especially if you play up front, because there's no expectations. You always get a goal, and I scored on my full debuts for Arsenal, Villa and Walsall. In his first ever professional game Tone had a shocker, but he got through it. Later, in the 1988 European Championships, he played for England in the group stages against Holland and was torn apart by Marco van Basten. It was horrible to watch, but he bounced back from that too. Even before the *Daily Mirror*'s 'Eeyore

How Not To Be a Professional Footballer

Adams' headline, the fans used to make donkey noises at him wherever he played, and while it gave him the hump sometimes, it never affected his game.

I knew Tone would pull through, even when he was later banged up on account of the drink-driving incident. But to be honest, I was just relieved it wasn't me in the shit for once. I'd had more than my fair share of naughty newspaper headlines. This time, I was out of the limelight. The calm before the storm, I think they call it.

Do Not Bet on Scotland on Your Wedding Day

'Merse's gambling binge begins, big style.'

An average afternoon in the Merse household, 1991, would be something like this. If it wasn't a Tuesday I'd leave the training pitch at 12 o'clock, have a shower and rush home by one. I was never one for hanging around, chatting with the others in the canteen. Once I was indoors, I'd sit on the sofa and put my feet up, but by three I was always bored shitless. I'd feel fidgety and edgy. Then I'd flick on Teletext, put my William Hill head on and everything would be all right again. Mate, I just couldn't sit still until I'd laid a bet.

It was the same old routine every day. At first, I'd pretend to take an interest in the football news and then 'accidentally' find the dog racing page, kidding myself that I was only having a look. After what felt like a million years, all the day's races would flash up with the race times and dog names, odds and form guides, so it was easy for me to pick a bet. One of the bookies would always run an advert on the bottom of the screen, bigging up their telephone service. I was straight on the blower.

'Yeah, £2,000 on trap four.'

Then I'd sit there again and wait. And wait. And wait. I couldn't be arsed to walk down to the bookies to watch the race. The dogs weren't shown on the telly back then either. My only option was to look at 'the poor man's Internet' and wait for the results to flash up. When they did, sometimes I'd win, most of the time I lost. I didn't give a toss. I'd always pick up the phone and chuck another couple of grand at the next race straightaway.

Two grand is a lot of money today, but it was a small fortune back then. Despite the big sums of dough flying around, I found that it was always easy for me to bet on the phone. Even when I was out of money I could call the betting shops and ask for credit. A lot of them would give it to me because of who I was and what I was. They knew I was good for the money eventually. That meant I could bet whenever and wherever I wanted, and for serious sums too. It was lethal.

My advice to any professional footballer thinking about getting a taste for online gambling today is: 'Forget it'. Betting out of a credit account is a lot different from going into a bookies and handing over thousands in cash. At that time I'd have definitely thought twice about putting a bet on if I'd had to go into a bank to draw out £10,000 in notes before filling in a betting slip, no matter what I was earning or what I was betting on. Later, as my habit got worse, that changed, but when I laid a bet over the phone with credit, it felt like I was spending Monopoly money. It didn't seem real, but I was a compulsive gambler and there was nothing I could do to stop myself.

I'd go through this same process every day. I knew I had a problem, because I couldn't stop and I loved the buzz of betting. What had started as a moment of madness with Wes in a Finsbury Park bookies was now a full-blown habit. I was chucking all my money away in bets: £3,000 here, £5,000 there; seven or eight grand on the horses. I wouldn't think twice about punting £10,000 on an NFL game in those days. The more money I earned, the more I gambled away, but I was such an addict, I even felt low when I won. One time when I was round my parents' house, I scored £20,000, I'm not sure what on, probably the curling in the Winter Olympics or something silly. Afterwards, I had face like a smacked arse. I was sulking. My mum couldn't believe it.

'My God,' she said. 'You've just won £20,000. You would have thought you'd lost by the look on your face.'

'Yeah,' I said. 'But there's nothing else to bet on now.'

I was fed up because the bookies had shut.

How Not To Be a Professional Footballer

She didn't understand, nobody did. I was always a moody person in the evenings until some years later when the US baseball was shown on the telly at silly o'clock in the morning and the bookies started running odds on the games. The Yankees, the Dodgers, the Mets – I became obsessed because I could feel the buzz all night.

My uncle later put it into perspective. He said, 'You gamble, what for? Whatever you win, whatever you lose, you're going to have the same dinner tonight.'

And he was spot on, I did always have the same dinner, but my addiction was never about spanking the bookies or making millions of quid and having a slap-up meal to celebrate. It was about the rush of chucking my money up in the air and seeing if it came back to me. Boozing kept up the high of playing, the feeling of excitement I got when I scored goals for the Gunners. Gambling stopped the boredom in the hours between training and games and the boozer. And because I had an addictive, compulsive personality (as my doctors in rehab would tell me), I took to it like a duck to water.

It screwed me up, though. Arsenal would win the League that year and I was about to make my England debut, but I was potless, and not because of George's tight pay structure at Highbury. Instead I'd spunked all my money in bets. Thousands and thousands and thousands a month had gone down the khazi on telephone gambling at home. It was so bad that when I moved into a new house in St Albans at the end of 1991, I had to sit indoors, freezing my bollocks off, because I had no money to buy a carpet. The central heating and electricity had been turned off because I couldn't pay the bills. I'd blown every last penny I'd earned. One week I was so skint I had to go round my mum's for something to eat. I couldn't even afford to buy a sandwich.

It was my own fault. The minute I started losing money, I'd start chasing – chucking more cash at the bookies to claw back the blown bets I'd made. It was the classic behaviour of a compulsive gambler, but I never learnt from my mistakes. When I first started making it into the Arsenal first team, I was betting two, three, maybe five hundred quid a time. By the time we'd won the League for the second time in 1991, the low bets were in the thousands. The more money I earned, the more I'd bet, it was as simple as that. If I won, I'd bet harder, only stopping when I was down to my last penny or the betting shops had shut up for the night.

I think the biggest issue was that nobody really knew what I was doing. Well, apart from Lorraine, who was going round the bend with the amount of money I was chucking away. She'd had to put up with it for years. Shortly after I'd been done for drink-driving in 1986, we had a blazing row. I'd spent the afternoon in a bookies and when I came home she was peeling spuds in the kitchen. An argument started because I'd lost a lorryload of money and had the hump. We started screaming the house down and I told her to where to go as I walked up the stairs to get changed.

Lorraine chased after me with the peeling knife. She was that fed up, and I couldn't blame her. She'd already had to deal with the Old Bill nicking me. Other times when I'd been out till all hours, I'd come home with mates and make a load of noise, shouting, taking the mickey. We'd first got engaged when I was 18, and for years the wedding was constantly on, off, on again, like our relationship, because I didn't know whether I wanted to settle down with her or go on the razz with the lads from the club. Now I was chucking all our money away.

'I've had enough,' she screamed at me, waving the knife around. 'It's either me or the betting.'

In my head there was no choice, I couldn't give up the love of my life.

'You'll have to go,' I said. 'I can't give up the betting, I love it too much.'

It wasn't the best thing to say, and Lorraine lashed out, slashing me across the hand with the blade. It tore my skin to shreds and I could see it was a bad one. She started crying, and while I was bleeding we patched up the row. I was driven to hospital and had 10 stitches put into my hand, but I knew I couldn't stop my gambling. Nothing was going to get in the way of me and a betting slip.

There wasn't a social occasion in the world that could stop me from putting a bet on. Lorraine and I got married slap bang in the middle of the 1990 World Cup, and on the day of our wedding I knocked back seven vodkas before I'd even got to the church. I avoided the lager tops because I didn't want to stink of a pub carpet in the church. Then I got my William Hill head on.

England were up against the Dutch that day and I knew quite a few of the boys at the ceremony wanted to watch it, but my mind was on Scotland. They were playing Costa Rica and, at odds of 2/7 on, I fancied a big flutter, so I got my best man to put a £500 bet on for me before I got hitched. I was up and running for the day. That night, I sat on the edge of the marital bed as Scotland were humiliated 1-0 by the worst team you'd ever seen in a World Cup. It was supposed to be the happiest day of our lives and I was gutted.

That year, our first son Charlie was born, but when Lorraine started having labour pains I freaked out. Rather than packing the overnight bag, calling relatives and getting her to the hospital, I told her to drive to the hospital on her own. I put a bet on and sat in front of the telly to watch the American football. It was the only way I could deal with the situation.

'Give us a ring if anything happens,' I said as she drove off.

Lorraine was fine, and according to the doctors she wasn't going to give birth that night. She'd felt a kick, but nothing more. When she got home, I was still in front of the telly, watching the final quarter. Maybe the doctors should have given *me* an examination that night instead.

Nobody could really tell when I was gambling. It was different from my other addictions. To get paro I had to drink lorryloads. Later, when I wanted to get high, I had to take drugs. To gamble I didn't have to physically put anything inside me. All I had to do was make a bet, whether that was by walking into a betting shop or ringing up a bookie, and bang, the money was over and I was on another crazy streak.

The thing that scared me most about gambling was that I could lose all my money overnight. That too was different from drinking. I knew that no matter how much I drank, I'd still have cash in the bank the next morning. I couldn't piss all my wages away in one night, it would have killed me, but I could blow all my money in one second with a bet.

Mixing the two was a nightmare, because any systems I had would go out of the window when I was smashed. I would wake up and not know how much I'd gambled the night before because I'd been so paro. It was terrifying, but gambling is a terrifying addiction. There are no immediate, physical symptoms, and people can't tell if someone has had a bet, unlike a drunk, who will stagger down the road when he's had a skinful. It's written all over his face.

I honestly think that gambling is the biggest problem that faces the modern footballer today. They can't go out and sink 15 lager tops. The minute a Premier League star walks into a pub, everyone starts posting the news online. Then the press start moaning: 'Oh, what'sname was drunk on a Tuesday night when he earns all that money, tut, tut.' I was lucky I could get away with it. No one was Twittering or Facebooking about me when I was crapping on Spunky's balcony or pushing Grovesy into the sea.

Drugs aren't in the equation these days, either. If a player starts snorting coke and he's caught out, then he's facing a massive ban. It's just not worth it. So that only leaves gambling as a vice (well, and women) and there's a hell of a lot of that going on. An international player could be online right now, blowing tens of thousands of pounds in bets, and nobody would know. The only people who see the betting big hitters are bookies, and they're not going to say anything. A Premier League footballer is a dream punter, because he's got money and time to burn. It's in the bookies' best interest to keep the names under wraps. It keeps them gambling.

Some of them get caught out. I've seen it with winger Matthew Etherington. When he was at West Ham he blew £800,000 in bets and was getting death threats because he couldn't pay up. Without naming names, I've heard of other Premier League players on telephone-number wages and they're in more debt than Etherington. I catch the gossip all the time: 'So-and-so is in trouble, he's blown everything, even though he's getting £120,000 a week. He's had to remortgage his house.' These are players that should have a gazillion quid in the bank. Instead they've got sod all.

It's all relative though really. It doesn't matter whether you're a footballer on telephone-number money or a milkman, if you're gambling more than you earn then it's a disaster waiting to happen. I could earn £2,000 a week and have the same problem as a milkman earning £300. If we gamble a tenner more than our salaries then we're both in shit. I was lucky, though. Back then I earned enough money to have a bet whenever I wanted. I didn't really have to beg, borrow or steal to put a wager on.

I was also very up and down with gambling. One minute I was the happiest bloke on the planet, the next I was the most depressed. Once, when a horse I'd backed big finished last, I booted a TV down the stairs in our house. The screen smashed into a million pieces as it hit the floor and Lorraine went mental. I sulked for the rest of the day.

Weirdly, it never affected my game. George would tell you: I never took my problems on to the pitch. As soon as it got to 3 p.m. on a Saturday and I was over that white line, all the pints and the bad bets were forgotten. Unless I was still drunk. Playing football was a release, it was the best high in the world, and while George might have had an idea about my betting, he wasn't that bothered while I was doing the business for him.

None of the other lads really knew I was blowing all my money. We'd always have a bet at the Arsenal, but it was nothing major. We usually chucked a few quid around a game of cards at the back of the bus, but that was about it. The other lads were very settled and balanced - well, most of them. Apart from me, the gambling back then was normal. Not that Lorraine felt that way.

George was gambling too, but unlike me, his wins were coming up big. After we'd struggled in the 1989-90 season, he shook up the midfield by taking Swedish winger Anders Limpar from the Italian club, Cremonese. He was quite a player, quick and very skilful. George then sold John Lukic to Leeds and signed QPR keeper David 'Spunky' Seaman and he was different class, too. Honestly, Peter Schmeichel - when he signed for Man

United in 1991 – and Spunky were the best goalies in the League by a million miles in those days. I was glad he was playing for Arsenal rather than against us.

I remember we'd faced QPR earlier in a Mickey Mouse competition called the Centenary Cup. During the game there was a break from midfield and I went up for a ball with their international defender, Paul Parker, who had a hell of a leap on him. This time he fell over and the ball ran free. I legged it from the halfway line towards goal with only the goalkeeper to beat, but then Spunky stepped off his line. I swear, the way he moved out, it made the target look like a hockey goal. It just shrank, and I couldn't see the Caspers on either side of him.

I always fancied my chances in one-on-ones with keepers, because all of them gamble at some point and dive at the striker's feet. That's when I liked to pop the ball over the top or nip round the side, but Spunky just stood there. I crumbled and fluffed my shot. I remember thinking, 'Bloody hell, he's good.' Pity I couldn't say the same when he started prancing around on *Celebrity Dancing on Ice*.

With David in goal, we were unstoppable. We only lost one game all season in 1990–91 and that was to Chelsea away. We were knackered with injuries that day and our defence was down to the bare bones. (We were so good at the back that we only let in 18 League goals all season, but I'm not having it that it was all down to the defence. As George was forever telling us, 'Defence starts from the front.') Against Chelsea, Bouldy got a knock in the game and George had to put Mickey in the back four because everyone else was in the treatment room. Mickey couldn't kick his way out of a paper bag normally, but we were that desperate.

We hammered teams as well. That season we put four past Chelsea at home; we battered Liverpool 3-0; we did Crystal Palace and Southampton 4-0 and scored five against Villa. On the last day of the season we smashed Coventry 6-1. People used to sing 'Boring, boring Arsenal' at us because of the way we defended, but that season we scored 74 goals in the League and won the First Division by seven points.

The other funny thing that year was our mass brawl against Manchester United at Old Trafford in October 1990. We did them 1-0 that day, with Anders Limpar scoring the goal, but the only reason people ever remember the match is because it kicked off between the sides when Nigel Winterburn went in with a naughty challenge on their full-back Denis Irwin. United reacted and Irwin and their striker Brian McClair put the boot into Nigel as he lay on the floor.

Everyone piled in, well, everyone apart from me. Punches were being thrown about, and I didn't fancy it one bit, especially not when the likes of Gary Pallister and Steve Bruce were involved for United. They were pretty scary blokes when they were tackling you fair and square;

How Not To Be a Professional Footballer

I didn't want to find out what they could do when they had the hump. I just stood on the halfway line as everyone started hitting one another. We were later docked two points for the ruck; United got one point knocked off. It didn't bother us, we still ran away with the League.

The only other blip that season, and it was a big blip, was Tottenham's brilliant midfielder, Paul Gascoigne. Despite eating all those Mars Bars, Gazza was tearing up trees in the FA Cup and Spurs were drawn against us in the semi-final. It seemed like he'd got them there on his own, he was playing that well, but Spurs were no mugs at the time. They had players like Gary Lineker, Vinny Samways and Gary Mabbutt in the team as well as Gaz. Because it was a London derby, the FA decided to play the game at Wembley, which was a ricket as far as I was concerned. I personally thought that playing the semi-final under the Twin Towers took the shine off the final – I still do. The FA Cup Final was the day, and everyone wanted to play at Wembley in that game, not the semis.

Spurs were double fired up for the game because they'd got it into their heads that we'd already had our suits made for the final. That was rubbish. We were confident of winning the double, but not that confident. Still, the rumour certainly seemed to give them an edge. In the first half we gave away a free-kick in front of our box. It was about 30 yards out, so it shouldn't have caused too many problems, but Gazza took one of the best dead balls I have ever seen, it was a worldy. It bent over our wall, dipped just before David Seaman could get his fingers on it and crashed into the back of the net. As it swerved over my head, I thought, 'What a free-kick, what a goal.'

Even though it was scored by the other lot, I had to admire it. Spunky was gutted, though. When we got in at half-time, 2–1 down, he started saying sorry.

'What for?' I said.

He reckoned his studs had got caught in the ground and he should have stopped it. I told him not to worry, though I probably wouldn't have been so soft on him if it had happened after the Nayim goal from the halfway line, which lost us the 1995 UEFA Cup Winners' Cup Final against Real Zaragoza, or the Ronaldinho free-kick that went over his head in the 2002 World Cup when England lost to Brazil.

In the second half we battered Spurs. Then Gary Lineker hit one and Spunky let the ball slip through his hands again. He thought it was such an easy catch to make that he took his eye off the ball before he had it under control. As he looked to where he was going to pass it next, it went right through his fingers. In the end, we lost 3–1.

We were all gutted. In those days, the FA Cup semi-final was the ultimate game to lose; and for us there was nothing worse than losing it to Tottenham. Spunky just had one of those days, which was a rarity because he never usually made rickets. That's what made him such a blinding goalkeeper. Under normal circumstances, I'd have bet on him any day of the week.

LESSON 6

Do Not Wax the Dolphin before an England Game

'Merse makes his international debut and drinks for England. Graham Taylor does not like that.'

I spent a lot of money chasing buzzes in my life, but booze and gambling couldn't match the rush of making my England debut in September 1991. Standing with the teams at Wembley felt phenomenal, and when I heard the national anthems playing for the first time I was higher than Amy Winehouse after a night on the tiles with Pete Doherty. Graham Taylor was the England boss and I'd been picked for a pretty special game. Our opponents were the new Germany, a mixture of mullets from the East and West following the fall of the Berlin Wall. I think Tone might have driven into that one, too.

How Not To Be a Professional Footballer

I'd already played for the England Under-21s, but it wasn't the same as playing for the seniors. Anyone could get a run out for the kids in those days, and the games seemed pretty pointless to me. Sometimes if I was called up, George would want me to pull out because he wasn't a great lover of us playing in meaningless friendlies (well, he was Scottish). He'd often ask his players to pull a fast one with a mysterious hamstring injury or a pulled groin. He figured it was better than risking a real injury for the next Arsenal match. In those days, the FA trusted the club doctors and they never had me independently tested. When I ducked out with a sick note, I got away with it pretty regularly.

The other reason I didn't play for the Under-21s as much as I could have done was because I hated flying and would often freak out on flights. I'd sweat, panic and get really nervous. I hated the thought of being up in the air and having no control over the plane – I still do. One time I even went to see Paul McKenna, the hypnotist, for help. I sat in his chair while he talked very slowly and deeply at me, but the treatment didn't really work. These days it's fifty-fifty whenever I book a holiday. Sometimes I can get on a plane with no problems, other times I jump off just before the flight taxis on to the runway. I'm so bad that for the last three days of a break abroad I can't sleep because I'm too worried about the trip back to England.

Do Not Wax the Dolphin before an England Game

So for that reason I never played a lorryload of Under-21 games, and if I did play, it was usually at home. But when I got my first call-up to the senior team, everything changed. Because it was a proper game, George was made up for me and encouraged me to go; the flying was something I was determined to struggle through because I wanted to play for my country so much (though it helped that my first game was at Wembley). Becoming an international footballer felt like a massive achievement, not just for me, but for my mum and dad as well. Having an England player in the family was a big, big deal. It wasn't such a big deal when we lost 1-0 to the Germans, but at least I got a run out, coming on as a sub in the second half.

I loved being in the England squad. There were some top, top players in there at the time like Gary Lineker, Chris Waddle, who was at Marseille, David Platt and Forest's Stuart Pearce. Gazza was injured that night, because he'd torn ligaments in his knee after trying to cut Nottingham Forest's Gary Charles in half during the 1991 FA Cup Final, so that particular meeting of minds would have to wait. I realised right then that England had a lot of quality players, it was just the manager who wasn't up to much. And the more I played for Graham Taylor, the weirder it got.

Tactically, he was all over the place. Before a game we'd often have to sit in the video room and watch an hour of the opposition taking throw-ins. Graham's thinking was that the team taking the throw was weakened, they only had 10 men on the pitch and we should take advantage. It all seemed a bit Mickey Mouse to me – they were a man down for all of one second – but that didn't stop him from making us watch years of videos.

Whenever it came to team selection he'd always stick to the same players. That was better than tinkering about, I suppose, but it also led to complacency among the lads who weren't playing regularly, especially me. I didn't need an excuse to muck about. When we played Finland away in Helsinki as a warm-up to Euro 92 in Sweden, Graham told the whole squad his preferred starting 11 for the tournament before we'd even got on the plane. Fair enough, he had every right, but with me that was a mistake. Knowing that I wasn't playing gave me another excuse to slack off. In the hours before the Finland match, when the squad was supposed to be sleeping, I sat up, watched the telly and waxed the dolphin. It was quite a nice afternoon.

In those days my ankles were like glass and I always used to have strappings on my lower legs to act as a support. I was terrified of them giving way, but that afternoon I didn't bother. I figured, 'Well, I ain't playing, what's the point?' In the dressing-room I pulled my tracksuit and boots on and sat on the bench, thinking I'd have an easy afternoon. Big mistake. After 10 minutes John Barnes ripped his Achilles' tendon and Graham told me to warm up.

'Shit,' I thought. 'My ankles are going to shatter in the first tackle and I'm knackered from waxing the dolphin all day, this is going to be a nightmare.'

Miraculously, I got through the game without injury or fainting from exhaustion, but it taught me a lesson. After that, I was always thorough in my pre-match preparation, whether I was playing or not.

Graham could make some weird decisions during games. When we finally got to Sweden, I was named as a sub for the third and final group match against the hosts. We'd already drawn 0-0 against France and the eventual winners Denmark, and in the last game we were drawing 1-1 with 25 minutes to play. A win would have got us through, but Graham decided to take off our leading striker and captain, Gary Lineker, which caused a right stink because he had a chance to equal Bobby Charlton's international goalscoring record of 49 goals (Gary had 48) and he'd announced his decision to retire from England duty after the tournament. His replacement, my Arsenal teammate Alan Smith, was a great player, but - no offence intended - he wasn't Gary Lineker. We lost the game 2-1.

Sometimes managers make strange decisions when they're under pressure. I remember watching Man City lose to Wolves while I was working on *Soccer Saturday* in October 2010. Even though they were 2-1 down, the City boss, Roberto Mancini, decided to replace his only striker, Emmanuel Adebayor, with a right-back. Now what's the thinking in that? I honestly reckon that, in those situations, the ref should stop the game, pull out a microphone and say to the manager, 'So, mate, what are you thinking here? Are you sure you don't want to change your mind?'

That's exactly what happened with Graham: he was under pressure against Sweden and he made a weird decision. People might say, 'Oh, but he showed bottle subbing Lineker,' but a manager shouldn't bring his leading scorer off if his side needs a goal. I was on the bench at the time and I remember the lads looking at each other in shock. Everyone was thinking the same thing: 'Oh my God. Subbing Gary Lineker? You can't do that.'

It was a strange one and no one was happy with Graham when we lost the game and England finished bottom of the group. The next day, the *Sun* ran a back-page picture which had Graham's face in the middle of a big old turnip. The headline read, 'Swedes 2 Turnips 1'. It went downhill from then on.

He became unlucky. In the qualification stages for the 1994 World Cup in America we had to play Holland. Now they were a pretty tasty team with Dennis Bergkamp and Marc Overmars in the line-up. At Wembley we went 2-0 up, but then Gazza broke his cheekbone and had to go off. Bergkamp got a worldy goal, then Holland nicked a penalty at the death after Des Walker had hauled down Overmars, who was lightning quick. We ended up drawing 2–2. When we played them in Rotterdam, it was even worse. I hit the inside of the post with a free-kick, and then Ronald Koeman – who should have been sent off for pulling David Platt down when he was clean through on goal – scored from a free-kick at the other end. We lost 2–0.

I suppose people make their own luck, and Graham hadn't helped himself because he'd allowed a Channel Four crew to film the action on the touchlines during the qualification stages. It was for a *Cutting Edge* documentary called *Graham Taylor: The Impossible Job*, although nobody knew it was going to be called that at the time. They nailed him. In Rotterdam the cameras captured him using his catchphrase, 'Do I not like that'. Then they made him out to be a bit of a mug when he'd started complaining to the ref and shouting at his players, particularly Sheffield Wednesday's Carlton Palmer, who had come in for a bit of stick from the England fans because he had the odd ricket in his locker.

It didn't look good. Yeah, he'd lost the plot a bit, but I thought it was a bit disrespectful – the people making the show had taken the mickey. The editors belittled Graham and then they made his coaches, Phil Neal and Lawrie McMenemy, look like a right pair of yes-men. I thought it was out of order on those two. It's always very rare for a number two to question the decisions of his manager in public, not if he wants to stay in the job, anyway. Phil Neal had won just about everything in the game (count them: eight Division One titles, one UEFA Cup, four European Cups, four League Cups, and the European Super Cup). All of a sudden he was a laughing stock.

I'd say one thing for Graham, though: throughout his time as England manager, he was great with the lads. If ever we went away with England for a week in a hotel, he'd always lay on something for us. Sometimes we'd go out for a meal as a squad, and when we got back he'd set up a suite with a mini casino for all of us to mess about in. He always made sure that the lads weren't sitting around in their rooms, bored shitless, but by giving me booze and a licence to gamble, he might as well have given me a loaded gun.

I learnt pretty quickly that if I wanted to get paro on England duty I should always hang around with the captains. Somebody like Tone or Incey was never going to be sent home if they'd been caught getting up to no good, it would have caused too much of a scandal. If I was drinking with the captains, I wasn't going to get binned either, because it would have looked like the manager had one rule for one person and another for me. Whenever I

Do Not Wax the Dolphin before an England Game

wanted to get on it, I'd always make sure I was with those two. It was like carrying my own 'Get out of jail free' card.

There was plenty of drinking to be done, England shirt or no England shirt. When it came to international duty, before a home game we'd always meet up in the team hotel at Burnham Beeches on a Saturday night. Graham often allowed us to have a drink in the bar. Some of those nights got very messy and I'd always get stuck into the beer. One session, a couple of days before a European Championship qualifier at Wembley, me and Tone really went for it. I went up to our room at three or four in the morning, leaving Tone with his pints downstairs. I'd gone up to call my wife, and when he finally came back, I was on the phone. The room was locked and he couldn't find his key, so he started banging on the door.

'Merse, let me in!' he shouted.

I was still on the phone to my missus so I ignored him and made out I was asleep. Bang, bang, bang! He kept knocking on the woodwork, but I kept blanking him. The next thing I knew, Tone had kicked the door in. It flew off its hinges and landed in the middle of the room. The door was followed by Tone, who was legless. We both stared at it for ages, before falling about laughing. Because neither of us had a tool kit – well, it's not the sort of thing you bring on international duty – we couldn't repair the damage, so somehow Tone just propped the door back up, balancing it on its hinges.

How Not To Be a Professional Footballer

The next morning we were due to get up for training, but the pair of us were still half cut. Tone got into the shower to shake off his hangover and I stayed in bed. Then somebody knocked at the door. I had my head under the covers and all I could hear was Tone shouting from the shower.

'Come in!' he yelled. 'Come ii-iinnn!'

He was laughing his head off, probably because he knew the door was away from its hinges and likely to fall down at any second. I creased up too, expecting someone like Incey or Gazza to send the door flying, but when I came out from under the duvet, Graham Taylor was standing over me. Then I heard Tone again, still in the shower.

'Merse, who is it?' he shouted. 'Merse? Merse!'

Graham looked from the broken door to me as Tone kept on shouting. He was shaking his head. It was obvious he'd got the hump.

'I'm not taking the blame for this,' he said. 'If this gets out, it's your problem, not mine.'

Then he left. Nothing more was said. When we came back from training, the door had been miraculously fixed, and nobody breathed a word of it to the press. It was like the whole thing hadn't happened. But it was like that with England in those days.

Do Not Wax the Dolphin before an England Game

At home Arsenal were doing their best impression of a team that didn't want to win a trophy. We'd already experienced that nightmare during the 1989-90 campaign when we'd defended the title without much joy. In '92 it was the same old story: we were nowhere near a pot, finishing fourth behind champions Leeds, Man United and Sheffield Wednesday in the old First Division. We also went out early in the League Cup, losing to Coventry City 1-0 away in the third round. I'm not making excuses, but that year we were spanked by injuries. What made it harder was the fact that everyone upped their game against us again. As I've said before, the matches were a lot tougher as champions. Everyone wants to beat you so much more. I've got respect for Man United because they can do it season after season.

It was in the FA Cup that we really made a bad name for ourselves. We lost to Wrexham in probably the biggest upset in the history of upsets. We were drawn away at the Racecourse Ground, but that really shouldn't have been a problem because we were such a good team. On paper it was a complete mismatch. They had finished bottom of the old Fourth Division the previous season and were somewhere around there at the time of the game. We were champions and still in the hunt for the League title when we met them.

We'd even strengthened the side from the previous campaign. George had gone out and bought striker Ian

Wright from Crystal Palace. Wrighty was some player. He used to destroy defences, slaughter them in fact. Often I'd wonder if he wasn't born to score goals. He'd bang one in during training and celebrate it like it was a winner at Anfield, and on the pitch he was as good as I'd seen.

For George, he was a godsend. Sometimes we'd be under the cosh in a game – one corner against us, then a second and a third, and it seemed only a matter of time before the other lot scored. Then, on the fourth, Tone or Bouldy would boot the ball up the pitch, Wrighty would get on the end of it, beat three players and pop a goal away. Whenever he did that I'd always think, 'Where the fuck did that come from?'

The other lot would be trudging back to the halfway line for the kick-off with a sorry look on their faces. I'd seen it countless times. It said: 'Well, we're screwed now, because we're not going to get two goals against the Arsenal.' I can't believe he didn't play a million times for England, because he'd make a goal out of nothing, but later, when he was still on fire for Arsenal, Teddy Sheringham and Alan Shearer were the preferred strikers for England.

Wrighty had a mouth on him as well as a scoring touch. He'd always gob off to defenders during matches, just to get under their skin and put them off their game. Most of them would leave the pitch with earache. I remember England defender Des Walker always had him in his pocket when he played for Sheffield Wednesday and Forest. He was a class act and Wrighty could never shrug him off, but that wasn't enough to stop him blabbering away.

'I'm going to get one chance, Des,' he'd say to him as the two jostled at a corner or a free-kick. 'You know I'm going to get one chance, Des. And I'm going to score from it.' The thing was, he always did. It used to drive Des crazy.

When he was mouthing off, Wrighty was the only player I knew who would back it up with his fists if he had to. Players would always give it loads during games, squaring up to one another and having a good old push and shove after a late tackle. They'd shout, 'I'll see you later,' but it was always bollocks, nobody ever had a punch-up. It's the same today. When players start going at one another, the ref should say, 'All right, lads, go on then, 30 seconds. Have a fight.' You'd see how quickly the arguing stops.

Wrighty was one of the few players who would see it through to the end. He'd go into the players' lounge look-ing for whoever had pissed him off during the game, then he'd square up and say, 'Come on then, let's go.' At Black-burn he went up to the Swedish striker Martin Dahlin and offered him out. He did the same to a lad at Norwich who was twice his size. Both of them crapped themselves. I couldn't blame them – Wrighty was a nutter.

If Wrighty had played against Wrexham, he would have scored 50 goals, no doubt about it. The fact that he wasn't playing was because he'd picked up about 30 bookings in the previous three games and was suspended. At half-time we were 1–0 up after a goal from Smudger but, to be honest, it could have been 100. I've never been in a more one-sided match. Even George didn't seem that arsed in his team talk; he knew we were bossing it.

'Right, no silly injuries,' he said. 'No sending-offs. Let's just get this game out of the way and get out of here.'

Then Wrighty started gobbing off. He'd come along to watch the tie.

'Fucking hell, if I'd been playing I'd have scored 20 by now,' he moaned. Then he shouted towards the Wrexham dressing-room. 'Why don't you Taffies start giving us a game? We've come all the way from London for this. You're wasting our time!'

In the second half we started battering them again, it was all too easy, but we couldn't score. Then, with 10 minutes to go, Wrexham got a free-kick about 25 yards out from Spunky's goal. The Welsh winger Mickey Thomas stepped up to take it, and we knew he'd been quite a good player in his day, turning out for Man United and Everton. He was 37 at the time and to be fair, I hadn't noticed him all game, it was that one-sided.

Mickey hit a beauty. I was in the wall and, like Gaz's free-kick at Wembley, the ball sailed over my head and crashed into the back of the net. All the lads looked at each another. I could tell everyone was thinking the same thing: 'Fucking hell, we're not going out on Tuesday now – there's going to be a replay.'

Everyone started arguing, we all had the hump because we couldn't get paro the following week at the Tuesday Club. A few minutes later, Wrexham scored again and Tuesday night was back on because we'd been dumped out of the FA Cup – but honestly that wasn't meant to happen. In the dressing-room George was furious, but he was so angry he couldn't speak. Even Wrighty didn't have it in him to shoot his mouth off. It was double embarrassing. We still went out on Tuesday and got paro like we'd wanted, but instead of celebrating and having a laugh, we were drowning our sorrows.

LESSON 7

Do Not Go to a Detroit Gay Bar with Paul Ince and John Barnes

'A summer tour to America descends into boozy chaos. Merse blows his chance of pop superstardom.'

When I went abroad with England I always found time to start a piss-up. Some of the players piled into the booze on international duty, especially after we lost away to Norway in the qualification stages for the 1994 World Cup. In our heads we weren't going anywhere under Graham Taylor. The team hadn't really got enough points at that stage to be certain of getting through (although it was still possible mathematically), and some of the results had been bad, like drawing with Norway and Poland at home.

Do Not Go to a Detroit Gay Bar . . .

When the FA took us away to the United States in June 1993 for three friendlies, not a lot of the players took it too seriously. What was supposed to be preparation for the following summer turned into absolute carnage, a right piss-up. I'd never been on anything like it in my life, not even with mates. The trip was more like a Club 18-30 beano than an international tour for the England team. And I loved it.

The football was rubbish, though. First of all we played the USA in Boston and got tonked 2-0. Now that was embarrassing. In those days you had to be seriously shit to get beaten by the USA, who were rubbish because they didn't have many players in the English leagues. Well, apart from Roy Wegerle, who played for Chelsea, Luton and Coventry, and Sheffield Wednesday's John Harkes. The only other person of note was their defender Alexis Lalas, and people only really recognised him because he had a ginger goatee beard that made him look like a crap rock star, which he was half the time.

I knew Alexis because he'd had trials at Arsenal. He was forever getting his guitar out in the bar of the Novotel in St Albans, where he was staying, and it was hardly the height of cool. He was actually a brilliant guitarist and a great lad, but Arsenal released him because he kept kicking people in practice games and George wasn't having any of that. Alexis hadn't forgotten it, and when he scored America's second goal of the game he ran towards the bench where I was sitting. He started pointing at me, a shit-eating grin plastered all over his face.

'Fuck off, mate,' I thought. 'Fuck right off.'

As he reached the touchline, he slid on his knees, waving at me and cheering. It was so embarrassing.

'Don't come near me,' I hissed. 'This is bad enough us getting beaten by you. Don't bring me into the equation now.'

He was about two feet away from my face, giving it large. I just looked away into the stands, mortified.

Graham was fed up with the result, because the press started to slaughter him again. The *Sun* hammered us with the headline, 'Yanks 2, Planks 0!', which pissed everyone off, but by the time we got to Washington DC, where we were due to play Brazil, everyone had calmed down because the hotel was so plush – huge rooms, luxurious beds, TVs in the bathroom, the works. I could watch my bets coming in on the sports channel while lying in the bath, it was great.

The first night we were there, all the lads met up in the bar for a drink. I got hammered again, but when everyone went to bed, I wasn't done. I needed more. So around one in the morning I wandered out of the hotel in my England tracksuit, turned left out of the car park and walked until I found the nearest dive bar. It was a rough old place. The jukebox was broken, the pool table was torn up and some bloke was even face down on the bar. For once I wasn't the most paro drinker in the place.

I sat there for a couple of hours talking bollocks to what'sname and left in the early hours, when I was well gone. As I staggered home, I bumped into two blokes, literally, just as they were about to go toe to toe in a punch-up. They were massive, the sort of people I'd have crossed the road to avoid on a normal day, but because I was sloshed I was full of peace and love.

'Come on, lads,' I slurred. 'It doesn't have to be like this. What are you arguing about? Come on ...'

They both stared at me.

'What the fuck are you doing, man?' snarled one of them, stepping towards me.

Some pushing and shoving kicked off, and as it threatened to turn really ugly, I turned on my heels and ran back to the hotel. The next morning, I went down for breakfast, bragging to Paul Ince, Carlton Palmer, Nigel Winterburn and Wrighty about my adventures in the bar and the late night peace-keeping efforts when, out of nowhere, unannounced, two FBI agents walked into the room. For some reason they wanted to give us an urgent safety briefing. The whole squad was taken into a meeting room, where a top-brass cop started spelling out the danger zones of the city.

'Gentlemen, we want to bring to your attention some serious safety issues that should help you during your stay,' he said. 'I'm telling you this now and I want you to listen to what I say as it is of the upmost importance. Whatever you do, whatever happens, do *not* turn left out of this hotel, because the chances are you will find yourself in big, big trouble. People go in there by mistake all the time and they do not come back. It is the murder hotspot of the city, and DC is one of the murder hotspots of the United States. It is a very, very bad place.'

Everyone turned around and stared at me, jaws on the floor. My stomach jumped somersaults and I don't think the strong coffees I'd just gulped down had anything to do with it. I'd had a near-death experience. According to the cops, it was a miracle I was still alive.

To celebrate, I got drunk again. That night I stayed in my room with Teddy Sheringham and Carlton Palmer, because I wasn't risking taking another pissed wrong turn and ending up in Murderland. Instead, we sneaked a crate of Budweiser into the hotel and played cards. As we gambled on three-card brag, we necked bottles of lager, throwing the empties against the wall and laughing as they smashed into pieces with a loud pop. Nobody bothered clearing up the mess.

A day or two later we drew 1–1 with Brazil, David Platt scoring our goal. It was a respectable result, so the following night the whole squad and coaching staff went out for a drink together. We ended up in a riverside bar in Georgetown, a little posh part of the city, and I got paro again, knocking back beer after beer after beer. On pint number one hundred and something, I staggered outside and climbed on top of a limo that had been parked nearby. I started dancing on it, setting the alarm off as passers-by stared at me. Graham Taylor sprinted into the street.

'You've got to get down,' he pleaded. 'Please get down, Paul.' But I wasn't having any of it. I stayed on there until I fell off, my head hitting the kerb.

The next day, he called me up to his hotel room. I knew I was in trouble, but to be honest I wasn't that bothered. I was out of control and didn't care.

'I've had enough, Paul,' he said, trying to scare me. 'I'm going to send you home.'

I knew he was bluffing.

'You can't, boss,' I said. 'That's stupid. If you send me home there's going to be murders because everyone will want to know why I've been sent home and you'll cop another hammering from the papers.'

I was right, Graham knew it too and he didn't send me back, which gave me another excuse to celebrate because I was having the time of my life.

When we flew to Detroit to play our final game of the tour against Germany in the Silverdome, I went on the piss with Incey and John Barnes. Detroit was a weird place, there were a lot of car plants in the area and everyone dressed a bit odd – dungarees, checked shirts, caps, but before all that stuff was fashionable. Just after midnight, we mistakenly ended up in a gay bar. I swear it was the only place still open, and we were so pissed that nobody noticed the distinct lack of birds and the fact that all the blokes were dressed from head to foot in denim. I thought the handlebar 'tache was a local trend. It was only when some geezer in a leather cap dropped to his knees in front of another fella onstage and started fiddling around that the penny dropped and we got out of there sharpish.

When we staggered into the hotel at 2 a.m., Phil Neal was waiting for us.

'I've seen you lads,' he said menacingly as we walked into the foyer.

But Phil knew he couldn't do anything. Graham couldn't do anything either. Nobody could, I was completely out of control and loving every minute of it.

Looking back, we all knew that Graham's time was coming to an end. In America the lads had taken advantage of his weakened position, some more than others, me more than most. It soon came back to haunt me, though. When Terry Venables started as manager, he kicked me out of the England set-up almost immediately. Graham handed in his notice shortly after we'd mathematically failed to qualify for the World Cup in November 1993, and Terry, who had done well at Barcelona and Spurs, took over the following January.

Do Not Go to a Detroit Gay Bar . . .

Everyone knew he'd been a Jack the lad in his time, so we all assumed that it would be quite relaxed when the squad got together before the game against Greece at Wembley in May. At first it was. When we gathered at Burnham Beeches, he allowed us to have a few beers in the bar, but I didn't leave until three in the morning. I think the tipping point might have been when I clambered over the bar and poured a pint for myself when everyone else had gone to bed. Terry got to hear about it in the morning, but he still picked me for the game the following Wednesday. I had a howler. We won 5–0, but I was worse than all the Greece players. The day after the match, Terry pulled me to one side.

'You won't get in the squad while I'm the manager,' he said. He'd probably heard of my reputation on England trips and wanted to see for himself how badly I misbehaved, which was pretty badly. Still, I was glad he'd been honest with me. There would have been nothing worse than playing well on a Saturday for Arsenal, only to stare at the next England squad on Teletext and think, 'Why ain't I getting picked?' It would have given me the hump.

Terry could see that I was a trouble maker. He probably didn't want me messing up his chances behind the scenes and, to be fair to him, he had a good squad without me. Euro 96 was coming up in a couple of years, and he probably reckoned on England doing quite well, especially as we were hosts and didn't have to qualify. So did I. The only thing was, I'd blown any chance I'd had of being a part of it. Still, every cloud has a silver lining. I now had plenty of time to get my drinking together.

The 1993 England beano in America came on the back of a seriously good season for Arsenal, and we scooped both the League Cup (or Coca-Cola Cup, as it was) and the FA Cup. It was also the first year of the Premier League, and although we finished in a disappointing mid-table position at 10th, in the Coca-Cola Cup and the FA Cup we were in dreamland. Those trophies were important to the players back then, definitely more than they are now, and in the Coca-Cola Cup I was having worldy games every other tie. Then, in the final, I played probably my best ever 90 minutes in an Arsenal shirt. We were up against Sheffield Wednesday and I had one of those matches where everything went right. I couldn't miss a pass, I was running past defenders like they were training cones. I used to get those matches sometimes; all players do. Whenever fans asked me what they were like, what I'd been thinking, I honestly couldn't tell them. I was in a zone. Everything happened instinctively.

We were one down when I scored a cracking goal that day, bang on 20 minutes. It was a beauty. I hit this shot so well that everyone thought the ball had taken a deflection, but it hadn't. Instead, I'd struck it flush and the ball swerved through the air and curved past their keeper, Chris Woods. To score under the Twin Towers was a dream. As a kid, in the park with my mates, I'd played that game 'Wembley', where everyone played everyone else in front of one goal. I loved the stadium. When I'd got one there for real, I was buzzing.

Later, I teed up the winner for Steve Morrow. The ball came out to me on the left wing and I skipped past Wednesday's full-back, my old Arsenal team-mate Viv Anderson. To be fair, Viv was about 91 years old by then, so he was never going to catch me. As I went past him, I crossed the ball in with my left foot. Carlton Palmer, who was playing for Wednesday, tried to control the pass as it went in, but he cocked up his first touch. He should have booted the ball away rather than being fancy. Stevie Morrow pounced on the loose ball and smashed it past Woods again. It was enough to win us the cup.

When the final whistle went, our celebrations turned into a right old fiasco. I ran towards the Arsenal fans, 'pulling a Merson', guzzling imaginary pints of lager and mugging up to the crowd. I don't know why I was showing off – I should have gone to the dressing-rooms in shame, because I looked terrible. I'd been to the hairdressers days earlier and asked for a 'wave', which was a slightly windswept style and had become the height of fashion at the time. I'd seen it in a magazine on Brad Pitt or someone, and it looked all right. It probably would have looked all right on me if the hairdresser hadn't given me a perm. Rather than looking like Brad Pitt, I looked like Cher after a night on the razz.

On the other side of the pitch, Tone ran towards Stevie Morrow, probably to thank him for the goal. He hoisted him up over his head, but because he was so excited, he slipped and dropped him on the floor, breaking Stevie's arm. I hadn't seen any of this happening when Ray Parlour ran over.

'Mate, Tone's picked up Stevie and dropped him,' he shouted. 'He's busted his arm and he's not in a good way.'

I looked over and saw Stevie in a heap. He was surrounded by physios, players and Tone, who was apologising big-time. I could see it was a bad one. Stevie's face was a pukey grey colour and his shoulder was at a funny angle. He was yelling in agony. We later found out that he could have lost his arm, the injury was that bad. Tone was beside himself in the dressing-room afterwards, he felt so guilty. It took him quite a few pints to get over it.

When we went to see Stevie a couple of days later, he'd been into surgery and was sporting a proper scar. There were so many stitches around his arm, it looked like Dr Frankenstein had pieced him together. I felt for him. Scoring that goal was the biggest thing that ever happened in Stevie's career, but most people only remember the 1993 Coca-Cola Cup Final because of what happened during the celebrations. I doubt Tone was his favourite person after that.

In the FA Cup we were doing just as well, having bombed past Yeovil Town. In the fourth round I scored one of my favourite goals, against Leeds at Highbury: they were 2-1 up and I got the equaliser with the last kick of the game. The ball got played down the wing to me and I cut inside, nipped past my marker and thumped it in. The ball hit the top corner. We took them to a replay and won at their place.

Just because we were playing well it didn't mean that we had to stop drinking. A few weeks later, we all got paro at Lingfield Park races and ended up in a nightclub called Ra Ra's. Tone got so smashed that he fell down a flight of stairs and busted his head open. When we beat Ipswich in the sixth round, I hung a cross up at the back post and Tone nodded it in. Everyone was jumping on him, but all I could hear was Tone shouting at the lads, 'Don't touch my head! Don't touch my head!'

Then it was dream time – we drew Spurs in the semi-finals. When the names came out of the hat, I knew we'd beat them because we were so fired up after the game in 1991. Spurs had probably banked on dining out on the Gazza match for a good decade or two, especially as we hadn't drawn each other in an FA Cup semi-final for a thousand years. Then it happened twice in quick succession and I had a feeling they wouldn't fancy it. I was right

– we won it 1–0, with Tone scoring the winner. The win set up another cup final with Sheffield Wednesday after they did Sheffield United 2–1 in the other semi.

Playing in the FA Cup Final was a weird thing. I grew up watching it all my life. I used to love the build-up before the match, watching *It's a Knockout*, *The Road to Wembley* and the coach journeys from the team hotels to the stadium. It was a really special day. My dad always had friends round to the house to watch the game, and an hour before it kicked off we all played football in the garden.

The closest I got to that excitement in 1993 was when we made a rubbish Cup Final single and *Top of the Pops* asked us to perform it on the telly a week or two before the game, which meant spending a night in the BBC studios in Wood Lane. I loved *Top of the Pops* as a kid, watching The Specials and Madness and all those ska bands, so I was all up for it, but when we met in The Gunners in the afternoon, which was a pub just around the corner from Highbury, it all went tits up.

We had a drink; I got stuck into the beers. Then one of the lads said, 'Right, we're off to *Top of the Pops* now,' and everyone else got up and ordered taxis over to the studio, but I couldn't be bothered. I was having too much of a great time getting drunk, so I stayed in the pub, played pool and got hammered. The following Thursday when *Top of the Pops* came on the telly, my missus got all excited. She was looking at the lads singing along in their club tracksuits, and was staring at all the players, trying to pick me out. I hadn't told her I'd been getting through a skinful in The Gunners at the time.

'Where are you?' she said.

'I dunno,' I replied, hoping she'd never cotton on. 'At the back somewhere, behind Dave Seaman and Tony Adams. They're so tall, them two, they've bloody blocked me out!'

When I actually played in an FA Cup Final, the day didn't have that feeling of excitement and novelty for me. I suppose it didn't help that we had to play Sheffield Wednesday again. We were sick to the back teeth of them, and they probably felt the same about us. On the day of the game, I got up in the morning, got on the team coach and drove to the ground like any other game. I didn't see any of the build-up because I was sat on a bus heading to Wembley, but I knew it was special because I felt double nervous.

I used to have a problem with going to the toilet when it came to big games. Often I'd get a nervous wee in the hours before kick-off. On a normal match day I could go five or six times in the dressing-room before we went out to play, but that day was even more nerve-wracking. It was the FA Cup Final, and all I could think about was the long walk to the pitch and the handshake with the guest of honour. I didn't want to wet myself in front of Wembley, not to mention the zillions of people watching all over the world. My bladder was in knots. Once we kicked off, I felt knackered.

Players who'd appeared in the FA Cup Final, whatever sort of club they were from, always talked about what a big pitch Wembley was to play on, especially at the old ground. Whenever I thought about that, I figured it was no bigger than a lot of the pitches I'd played on in the First Division, plus I'd been there with England and played in the League Cup Final a month earlier. I thought the FA Cup would be the same, but the first run I made from the kick-off changed my mind. I thought I was running in cement, my legs felt so heavy it was untrue.

It probably went some way to explaining why I had such a shocker. It was a crap old game, we drew 1-1, and I had a nightmare, an absolute shitter. I couldn't do anything right. Ian Wright scored one for us in the 20th minute, and then David Hirst equalised in the second half.

The replay wasn't much better. Neither team could get going, probably because we were falling asleep at the thought of playing each other again. It was pissing it down with rain as well. Ninety minutes couldn't divide us, and as the game crept towards the end of extra time at 1-1, all I could think was, 'Fucking hell, I really don't want to have to take a penalty here.'

Moments later, we got a corner and I threw in a cross. It was hardly a worldy, but for some reason Chris Woods didn't come for the ball. Our defender, Andy Linighan, got on the end of it and headed it home, and we ground out the win in the closing minutes. We'd won the bloody cup. I couldn't believe it. We hadn't deserved to win that game, not in a million years.

The match had dragged on for so long that by the time we got back to Sopwell House, Arsenal's hotel, the bar was shutting up shop. God knows what happened after that. All I know for sure is that I got pretty paro. My only memory afterwards was drinking with Bouldy at nine in the morning – brandy and Becks for breakfast. That was probably the highlight of the FA Cup Final for me, even though it was a game I'd dreamt of playing in all my life. Sometimes the things you dream of as a kid don't live up to the hype.

After our 1993 cup success and Graham Taylor's jolly boys' outing in America, I thought about getting back on the straight and narrow. During pre-season I worked my bollocks off and sweated and puked my way through all of George's running drills. I gave piggybacks up and down the North Bank and worked myself hard in practice games. Because of my international drinking I had to work on fitness more than most of the lads, but I was sharp by the time the 1993–94 season came around. If someone had asked me how I felt about the prospect of another year in the newly christened Premiership, I'd have given them one answer: 'Buzzing.'

How Not To Be a Professional Footballer

Our first game was against Coventry at home and I was up for it, everyone was, and on the Friday before the game, when George named me in the team, I was well excited. Too excited. Afterwards I met up with my mate Paul, and we went to a betting shop in Colindale, north London. We used to go in there all the time. I spunked a few quid on the horses and Paul asked me if I fancied a pint in the pub over the road to help me forget about the loss.

'No, I've got a big game tomorrow, mate,' I said. 'I want a good night's kip.'

'Come on, Merse,' said Paul. 'One won't kill you.'

He was right, I knew it wouldn't, but one pint plus another 20 did. I staggered out of there at five in the morning. I'd had three hours' kip when I turned up at Highbury looking like a dog's dinner. George could tell what had happened just by looking at my face, but he still played me. It was a mistake, because I was shocking. At half-time Coventry were trouncing us 3–0 and their striker, Micky Quinn, had scored a hat-trick. I'm not being horrible, but Micky was hardly Diego Maradona.

George took me off and I sat on the bench during the second half, feeling sick. After the game he tore into me with the whole team watching.

'You see him over there,' he yelled, pointing at me. 'I don't know how you can fucking look at him. He was out all last night pissing it up.'

Do Not Go to a Detroit Gay Bar ...

He binned me for the next game, but it was the beginning of another end for me. Several months later, in February 1994, the club received a letter. Someone claimed I'd been spotted scoring drugs in a boozer in Borehamwood, in Hertfordshire. George read it out to me in his office.

'Dear Arsenal Football Club,

'I am writing to you about the behaviour of one of your players, Paul Merson, who I spotted buying drugs in my local pub. His behaviour was unacceptable, especially for someone representing a professional football team. Blah, blah, blah ...'

He waved the letter in front of my face.

'So? Is this true?' he said.

I used the excuse I always pulled out for these occasions. 'It's Spurs fans having a laugh,' I said. 'Or somebody mistaking me for someone else. Remember that time when they said I'd been pissed in a nightclub in town when we'd all been away?'

George nodded. He had to ask me personally, because there were no drugs tests in those days. He could hardly get me to pee in a bottle, and he couldn't prove me wrong either, it was my word against the person who had written the letter. He bought the story, apologised for bringing it up and let me go. Then I went out and scored some more cocaine.

Do Not Wander Round Nightclubs Trying to Score Coke

'Merse loses the plot to Class A drugs.'

Cocaine absolutely, 100 per cent, brought me to my knees. I'd already downed about 100,000 pints of lager top and spunked away millions of quid at the bookies, but that was nothing – it wasn't going to kill me. Coke took away my life for 10 months and nearly finished me off. I could have quite easily snuffed it from a heart attack on the pitch, given the huge piles of stuff I was shovelling up my hooter. Once I'd started taking it, I couldn't get enough, and nothing was going to stop me from getting another line.

Do Not Wander Round Nightclubs ...

My habit got so bad that I'd get home from training, draw the curtains and sit in the dark, a couple of piles of white powder chopped out on the table in front of me. Teletext's dog racing page was on hold and my bookie was on speed dial.

I'd bet, and snort a line.

Bet, snort a line.

Betsnortaline.

Betsnortalinebetsnortalinebetsnortaline.

If the gasman had knocked on the door to read the meter, or a mate had turned up at the house unexpectedly, I would have crapped myself. I was so screwed up in the head that the slightest noise gave me the fear.

I don't know how much I'd spent on cocaine, I was so off my face when I bought it, I couldn't keep up with how much I was doing. What I do know was that I once owed a dealer £400 for a night's worth of gear. I was going out on benders three or four times a week, depending on how often Arsenal were playing. It didn't need Professor Stephen Hawking to work out a Theory of Misery to realise that I was spending shedloads of money on lorryloads of drugs and heading for the universe's biggest black hole.

I took my first line in February 1994, at a boozer called The Mousetrap in Borehamwood. At the time it felt like fate had pushed me there, because I'd honestly gone into that pub by mistake. I'd agreed to meet a mate of mine for a drink, and when he didn't turn up, I realised we must have been talking about different pubs. This was a time before mobiles, remember. I could hardly call him and find out where he was. I was flying solo for the night with my drinking head on and I definitely wasn't going home. There were loads of Arsenal fans around and they all wanted to buy me beers, so I stayed for a few. I was like a pig in shit.

Out of nowhere, one of the geezers I was with offered me some coke. It was a surprise, but I'd been around it a bit, mainly because I'd seen people in pubs doing it, or heard about people having it at parties, but it had never interested me at all. I wasn't clued up on it and I thought it might send me on a trip I couldn't get out of. I didn't want to be seeing flying elephants for the rest of my life.

'No, mate,' I said. 'I don't want none.'

That was the God's honest truth, but for a week afterwards I couldn't get The Mousetrap out my head. I'd say stuff to myself like, 'Oh, I liked that pub,' or 'I'm going back to The Mousetrap next Saturday night.' But why did I like that pub? Why did I want to go back to The Mousetrap? It wasn't a particularly nice boozer, there were another hundred and one pubs I could have gone to for a pint. Deep down I knew I was kidding myself. Deep down I knew I'd made up my mind to get on the coke and there was nothing I could do to stop the inevitable. It's the curse of having an addictive, compulsive personality.

Do Not Wander Round Nightclubs . . .

The following weekend we played Everton away and I scored a worldy goal against Neville Southall, chipping him from outside the box. I was made up and knew I was going to celebrate hard that night, because George hadn't been playing me much at the time. I'd been off form and feeling down about it, so playing and scoring again felt like a massive release. The minute the team coach pulled into the training ground car park, I was in the car and driving to Borehamwood. Then I ordered the first lager top in My New Favourite Boozer.

At first I didn't see the bloke who had offered me cocaine the previous week, so I didn't think about doing it. Later, when I clocked him, I felt a rush of excitement. We got chatting about the game, my goal against Neville; then he asked me if I wanted a line of charlie and I nearly bit his hand off. We went into the toilet and locked ourselves in the cubicle. He scooped out a pile of white powder and chopped it out on the top of the cistern, cutting it into lines with a credit card. I felt nervous, I thought about the damage it might do to my brain for all of one second, and then I got stuck in.

It's funny, when I think about that moment – that second where I'd first stuck a rolled-up tenner into my nose and sniffed my first line off the top of a pub khazi – I should have known it was a death sentence. Coke was going to take over my life, because everything I ever did was all or nothing: football, gambling and drinking, I didn't do anything by halves. I remember driving back from training with Spunky only a few weeks before my first night on the drugs and he'd asked me if I'd fancied popping in for one pint.

'One?' I said. 'What's the point in that? No thanks, mate.'

'Why the fook not?' he moaned.

He couldn't get his head round the fact that I never really drank for enjoyment like he did, like normal people did. I drank to get pissed. Once I started, I couldn't stop until I was unable to drink another drop. I knew that one pint was always too much and 100 pints were never enough. Everything about my personality was compulsive. Sniffing my first line of cocaine was absolutely the worst thing I ever could have done.

I snorted it up and my heart pumped at a million miles an hour. I didn't feel amazing, but as I walked back to the bar I felt double confident. I wanted to talk to complete strangers, which was unusual for me because I was quite a shy bloke when I was sober – I had been since I was a kid. I didn't like talking to people I didn't know and I was hardly Mr Big Bollocks in conversation. I once went out with a girl for eight weeks and didn't have the courage to kiss her in all that time, that's how reserved I was.

That night, though, I was on fire. I had another line and then another and there were no flying elephants. Instead, the stuff gave me extra drinking legs. I could pour pints and pints of lager top down my neck and it didn't seem to affect me. By the time I'd left the pub, it was silly o'clock in the morning, but I was wide awake, and when I woke up later that lunchtime I was still as chirpy as you like. I should have been hanging, hiding from the daylight under the duvet. That day I could have skipped through one of George's training sessions no problem. It was the best morning after in the world. It was also the worst: I wanted to get stuck into another line straight away.

That was it, the honeymoon period was over. It lasted all of one night. When I went to The Mousetrap the following weekend, and the weekend after that, and the weekend after that, I didn't notice anything different about myself. Well, apart from the fact that I was now buying a couple of grams a night rather than sniffing up handouts. When I'd started going in there during the week, I kidded myself that I was enjoying being part of a new crowd, even though I was hanging around with blokes I didn't know from Adam. I couldn't admit to myself that I was already an addict.

Everyone else could see it. It was obvious, because when I bought coke, I put it up my nose as quickly as I could. Some people in The Mousetrap could buy a gram and make it last all night. Other people only did it once a week, or once a month, but not me. I'd buy one gram and take a couple of big hits straightaway. Moments later I'd be at the bar, fidgeting because I'd want to have another. People would stare at me as I chopped out huge lines in the toilet.

'Oh my God,' they'd say. 'You can't take it like that, calm down.'

I wasn't listening, though, I was chasing the buzz. I was following it like a bad bet, which was a massive problem. I loved betting in the morning. The thrill of putting down the first wager was what got me going for the day. I was in a state of excitement waiting for the result to come in. But once I lost money, I'd bet more and more to make up for what I'd already thrown away. That was one of the symptoms of being a compulsive gambler. Cocaine had a similar effect. With the gear I was chasing the rush of excitement that came with my first ever line.

On heroin, junkies chase the dragon; after the first hit it's never the same again. Apparently it's always the best. It was the same with coke. Nothing matched the first time, but because I was addicted, I couldn't stop running after it. It was horrible, nothing about it was enjoyable, and it trapped me the minute it was pumping round my heart and veins. My life was fast becoming a waking nightmare.

When the pub was shut or I was at home alone, I'd sit in darkness and get through wraps and wraps, the little paper envelopes that dealers would give me every time I paid them a visit. Each wrap had a gram in it. In the evenings after chucking-out time, I would get a cab to Smithfield Market in the City. There was a pub there that was always open, so the traders could have a drink. Like alcoholics and druggies, they worked funny hours. I'd get off my face at the bar all night on more pints of lager, I'd snort coke in the toilet, and then I'd hail a black taxi to the training ground at six or seven in the morning. During the journey, I would open up a bag of white powder and stick my nose into it.

The geezer in the front would always stare at me through his rear-view mirror, jaw on the deck. I could see him thinking, 'Bloody hell, Paul Merson is doing drugs on my back seat.' I must have looked like the strangest thing in the world. I had a few cabbies say to me, 'Mate, what the fuck are you doing?', but they couldn't do anything. As I'd shown with those letters to Arsenal and George, it was their word against mine, nobody could prove a thing. If one of those fellas had gone to the papers and said, 'I had that Paul Merson in the back of the cab the other day and he was going through the Colombian marching powder like nobody's business,' who would have believed them? Any editor worth his salt would have said, 'Hang on, mate, how? What? Where's the proof?' Thank God mobile phone cameras weren't around in those days, I'd have been screwed.

How Not To Be a Professional Footballer

Once I'd got to the training ground, I was taking an even bigger risk. Even for a fit, healthy person, the training sessions with George always seemed like a death sentence, what with all that running about, all day, every day. As an alcoholic with grams and grams of charlie in me and a compulsive gambling addiction playing on my nerves, I was being man-marked by the Grim Reaper every time I pulled on my football boots. Oh my God, I'm lucky to be alive.

When the drugs ran out at home, I'd do anything to get my hands on another load. One evening, in the summer break, after I'd been sitting around the house all day, gambling, drinking and getting on the coke, I emptied out my last wrap and hoovered it up. I knew I needed more. It had been a hot spring day, and I'd been slobbing it around the house, not moving from the sofa, dressed only in my shorts and flip-flops. I looked like a dog's breakfast, but I had to get out, I had to score.

'I need some gear, I need some gear.' It was the only thought in my head as I drove round to the Middlesex and Herts Country Club, which was a fancy disco round Harrow way. Even though it was a top-drawer place, where the girls were dolled up to the nines and the blokes were dressed head to foot in designer labels, I showed up in my Bermudas and flip-flops. Ordinarily they wouldn't have let someone looking like that through the door, but the bouncer recognised me, and when I gave him a cock-and-bull story about needing to give someone their house keys he let me through.

'I'll only be a second,' I said.

For the next 20 minutes I wandered around the dance floor, looking like a nutter, asking people for drugs or the name of a dealer.

'Got any gear? Got any gear?'

I squeezed between cuddling couples and groups of girls dancing round their handbags.

'Got any gear? Got any gear?'

People were doing double takes. Lads, probably Arsenal fans, were pointing.

'Anyone got any coke?'

Jeremy Beadle the comedian was big at the time, playing pranks on people for the telly. I swear people must have thought he was going to pop out at any second, complete with a camera crew – it would have looked that weird. Come on, I played for Arsenal and England, it couldn't have looked any stranger. I was staggering around, red in the face and sweaty, and with a runny nose. I looked in a right state. When I struck lucky and found a fella with some cocaine, I bought a couple of grams. Then I went home and got even more off my head.

How Not To Be a Professional Footballer

I was playing all right for Arsenal at the time. It wasn't like I was washed up or coming to the end of my time in the game when I started on the heavy stuff. I wasn't trying to shut out the disappointment of a failed football career by doing coke. That would have made the situation slightly more understandable. Mate, I was in my prime, which made my drug problem even more self-destructive.

On the pitch, George had got us playing well again during the 1993-94 season, in Europe at least. In the League we couldn't turn the draws into wins and we were relying on Wrighty too much for goals. We got knocked out of the FA Cup (by Bolton) and the League Cup (by Aston Villa), both in the fourth round, but in the UEFA Cup Winners' Cup we were flying.

The funny thing about our European run was that we never went to anywhere extraordinary. The draw never sent us out to Outer Mongolia or the United Republic of Whatever. Instead we went to France, Belgium and Italy. We started off in Denmark against Odense BK and beat them 2-1. I scored one of the goals, and when the final whistle went, me, Nige and a few of the other lads did the Madness dance in front of the fans, the one where the whole band lined up one behind the other, bending their elbows and leaning backwards.

I wasn't so happy after the next leg. The bookies had put us in at 1/7 on to win at Highbury, and I thought that was the biggest dead cert in the history of dead certs. I was so confident we'd spank Odense that I put on seven grand to win another grand. They were absolute toilet and I thought we'd batter them. I honestly felt like I was stealing money with that bet. We went 1-0 up and then, at the death, the Danes scored an equaliser. In the dressing-room all the lads were as happy as Larry, jumping around and celebrating because we'd got through 3-2 on aggregate, but I sat there feeling sick. I'd blown another lump of money.

'Why did I do that?' I kept saying to myself. 'How did that happen?'

I honestly thought my bet was a certainty, I thought I was being clever. I was never superstitious about betting on myself (but I'd never bet on myself to lose, not in a million years). There was nothing better, because at least I knew I was trying my hardest to get a win. The result was in my hands, which was the perfect situation as far as I was concerned. Well, unless we'd leaked an equaliser against Odense.

We took Standard Liège 3-0 away in the next round, and then we thumped them 7-0 at home. It was probably the best team performance I'd ever been involved with at Arsenal – they couldn't live with us. Arsenal had been playing a 4-3-3 system under George, and everything just clicked. We were having fun in Europe and we didn't fear anybody. Against Torino in the quarter-finals we played at the Stadio delle Alpi in Turin, the ground where Gazza had cried against West Germany during the 1990 World Cup finals. When I saw the draw I remember thinking, 'That's a lovely game to play in.' I didn't care about how good or bad their team was.

When we got there, we were more like the St Trinian's hockey team than a Premier League football club, we were that excited. There was a massive speaker that hung down over the centre circle – if you ever watch Italian football on the telly, you'll see it. Announcements and doorbell tunes blare out of it all game. Our warm-up that night was to try and hit it with as many shots as we could. The Italians looked at us like we were mad. They must have thought, 'What the fuck are this lot like?' as ball after ball sailed up in the air, but no one got close to booting it down.

We drew 0–0 – it would still be 0–0 now if the ref hadn't blown for full-time, it was that dull a match. It was also a tough fixture, because Torino were very well drilled defensively, and we only got past them in the home leg 1–0.

Even so, some people had started knocking our results. They were moaning, saying, 'Oh, but it's only the UEFA Cup Winners' Cup, it's a bit Mickey Mouse.' They didn't know what they were talking about – the semi-finals had some proper teams in the draw. As well as us, there was Paris St Germain, Benfica and Parma. Real Madrid, Bayer Leverkusen, Torino and Ajax had been knocked out in the quarters. Honestly, I watch the UEFA Cup now and I haven't heard of half the teams in there. I knew of all the clubs we were playing in the UEFA Cup Winners' Cup and there were some tidy outfits, but I fancied our chances all the same. After the Odense disaster I wouldn't have staked my life on it, but I reckoned we could do a job against just about anyone.

Arsenal pulled Paris St Germain in the semis, and for the first leg we travelled to the Parc des Princes stadium, where David Ginola was playing merry havoc for their lot. It was down to me and Bouldy to deal with him at set-pieces, especially when he went down to the near post at corners. That's where George reckoned he'd been doing some serious damage, winning flick-ons and scoring goals. At corners, my job was to stand in front of him, Bouldy would tuck behind, and between us we would give him some serious needle.

'You big-nosed git,' I'd call him.

'What you going to do now, big nose?' said Bouldy when the ball went over his head for the 100th time.

I was dishing out loads, but don't get me wrong, I never called him ugly. He would have laughed in my face. To be fair to him, he took it all, and when a ball came in, David eventually got up above me and Bouldy and got a flick-on which went past Spunky and into the goal. Straight away, he ran away to the crowd, then all of a sudden he stopped.

'Wait there a minute,' he must have thought. 'I've got some unfinished business.'

He turned around and ran straight up to me and Bouldy, shouting his head off, giving it big-time. We'd asked for it really, but George was happy to take a 1–1 draw back to Highbury. I wasn't though, it was April and I had my cocaine head on, I was doing lorryloads. The Monday before our home tie, I went out and got off my face. I was wrecked for the rest of the week and my throat felt like sandpaper. I later picked up tonsillitis.

If I'm being honest, I could still have played quite easily, as it was a Thursday night game, but my head was a paranoid mess. In the days before the match I thought, 'I can't afford to play here. They have random drugs tests in European competitions. If I get picked out for one afterwards, I'm not sure I'll be able to make it.' Even though George really wanted me to play that game, I called in sick and watched the boys from home.

We won 1–0, which gave us a 2–1 victory on aggregate, but as I watched I knew I'd blown my chance of making the final against Parma in Copenhagen. George was quite a loyal manager and he pretty much always stuck with the teams that had got him to a cup final. So I knew that, on paper, I was being left behind. But later on in the game Wrighty picked up a yellow card, and because he'd already been booked in a previous round, it meant he was going to miss the final. I was gutted for him, he was such a great player and deserved to be there in a European final, but I knew his disciplinary record had got me back into the team.

If it had been down to form, I wouldn't have been lining up against Parma. The gear had affected my performances. I could still train and play, just not as well as previous seasons. Even though I was up all night, I could keep up with the training, just. I wasn't the fittest geezer in the world anyway, and I wasn't one of those players who would train hard all week – I just didn't like it. I liked the football, but I didn't like the running around. That's probably why George didn't put two and two together at the time. I was always strolling round the training ground with my hand on my cods; it was business as usual as far as he was concerned. Because I was losing a lot of weight due to the late nights and a loss of appetite caused by the drugs, I actually looked quite trim, even though I was weakening by the month.

George was down on his luck with injuries and suspensions, so he had to pick me, half-cocked or not. Wrighty was out, as was our midfield workhorse, John Jensen, who we'd relied upon during the season to battle us to points. He'd signed for us in 1992 from Brondy and had strengthened our midfield, but he couldn't score for toffee. He played 97 games for Arsenal and only bagged one goal. Our line-up that day featured Spunky, the famous back four, Paul Davis, Steve Morrow and Ian

Selley across the midfield, plus me, Smudger and Kevin Campbell up front.

It was a big ask to get a win against Parma that year, because they were a serious team. In fact, the experts were so confident we'd lose that when we arrived at the Parken Stadium in Copenhagen, the ground staff were positioning the winner's podium on the sidelines. We noticed it already had Parma written on it. On paper, it was probably a fair assumption. Tomas Brolin, Gianfranco Zola and Tino Asprilla all started for them up front, and all of them were worldy players.

It all changed in a heartbeat. Smudger got a class goal for us on 20 minutes. One of their defenders tried to boot a ball clear with an overhead kick, but he made a ricket and Smudger banged the ball past their goalie with his left peg. After that, Parma carved us apart. I honestly don't remember us getting another chance. Zola took a free-kick that blew my mind. He was 20 yards out and somehow he flicked the ball over the wall and down towards goal. It went just over the bar and landed on top of the net. I thought, 'How the fuck do you do that?'

Somehow we clung on and managed to get our name on the winner's podium. Clearly, Parma and UEFA hadn't realised that when teams went one down against Arsenal, it was tough for them to get back into the game. I think that was the first match I ever heard our fans sing, 'One nil to the Arsenal.' They went out and got smashed in

Do Not Wander Round Nightclubs ...

Copenhagen that night, but there was nothing in the way of celebrations for us. Arsenal were as tight as a drum. The club weren't going to lay on any parties or champagne receptions, plus George wanted us to be razor sharp for the last game of the season the following Saturday, which was against Newcastle away. We were given the next day off, but I knew I wouldn't play because Wrighty was available for selection. I took it as another excuse to close the curtains at home, turn on Teletext and get off my face.

LESSON 9

Do Not Get So Paranoid That You Can't Leave the House

'Out of his mind on drugs and booze, Merse gets double edgy. The walls begin to close in ...'

The more cocaine I sniffed up, the more paranoid I got. Every time a stranger walked up to the front door, I'd panic. If a car I hadn't seen before was parked outside in the street, I'd get the fear and hide in the house. For all the confidence it gave me whenever I took it, the drugs had turned me into a terrified and nervous recluse. Paranoia was a side effect of getting high that I couldn't handle.

I used to live a couple of miles away from the training ground, and in my car I could fly into work in under 10 minutes on a good morning. After I started snorting coke in the loos at The Mousetrap, that journey took me well over an hour. I'd go mental on the road. If a car was behind me for longer than a minute, I'd get it into my head that I was being followed by a drug dealer, a blackmailer or an undercover copper. Sometimes I'd imagine the person behind me wanted to kill me, so I'd pull over and do a U-turn. When I thought I'd lost whoever was apparently trailing me, I'd continue on to training before someone else popped up in my rear-view mirror, and then the horror would start all over again. I did more double-ups in my motor than Jack Bauer in an episode of *24*.

It was worse when I was at home. The road I used to live on had two houses in it, and both of them were protected from the street by a big iron gate. It was a busy road and cars used to pull up every now and then, but if ever I clocked one I didn't recognise, I'd imagine a dealer with a baseball bat or a tabloid journalist knocking on the door, both of them demanding money or answers. When somebody was at home with me, I'd send them down to the street to find out who the motor belonged to. I thought they were waiting for me, my brain was that messed up. Whoever was in the house with me at the time must have thought that I'd gone mental, because they had no idea I was on drugs. If I was sitting indoors on my own, I'd go to the back of the house and pray that the person in the car wasn't about to walk up the drive.

The stress was getting to me on the pitch, too. During matches I'd look up into the crowd and see all these faces staring back at me. I'd think, 'Who knows? Who's going to know? When are people going to find out?' I'd walk out with the teams and say to myself, 'Shit, I can't play too well today. What happens if I get man of the match, or score a worldy and I'm all over the back pages tomorrow? Someone I've been doing drugs with might go, "Hang on, I was snorting coke with that bloke in a pub last week, I didn't know he was a footballer." Then he might grass me up. Oh my God.'

Then I'd have nightmares: the people I'd imagined finding out about me were on the phone to the papers, they were selling stories on me. It was crackers. I knew it was all made up in my head, but that didn't make it any easier to stop the never-ending nightmares and freak-outs. I couldn't face the real world. I didn't want to walk along the street. I was living in an imaginary prison, and the bars had been put there by cocaine.

I was so nearly caught out. In the pre-season campaign for the 1994–95 season, George took us all to Sweden for some friendlies. We'd always train in the morning, and then the squad would have lunch together in a big banquet hall in the team hotel. That's when the messing about and the gossiping always started. One afternoon, Lee Dixon was banging on about his mate who worked for the *News of the World*.

'They've got a massive story on a Premiership footballer,' he said. 'He's been up to loads of bad stuff and they've been trailing him for months. He won't tell me which player it is or what he's doing, but apparently when it breaks, it's going to be massive.'

For some reason, despite my over-eager imagination, I never thought it could be me.

'Fuck, can you imagine who that is?' I said. 'I wonder what they've been doing?'

I never once, in my worst nightmares, pictured that I was the player Lee was talking about it. I'm not 100 per cent sure it even was me in the end, but when my problems were later all out in the open, I was told I'd been followed for months, just like Lee's mate had said. It made sense: an Arsenal and England player doing cocaine was just about as big a tabloid story as anyone could think up.

It wasn't just the papers that were closing in on me. People at the club were starting to take notice, too. One morning, when I came back from another Smithfield Market bender, I put away a couple of liveners in the back of the taxi. Midway through training, I went over on my ankle in a tackle and it swelled up like a boxing glove. It was huge. Because the coke was pumping around my body so quickly, all the blood had rushed to the injury. It looked pretty bad. Our physio, Gary Lewin, checked out the swelling and then glanced up at me. I could tell he knew that something was up, though even he probably wouldn't have imagined the truth.

How Not To Be a Professional Footballer

A few months later, when it all came out in the press, he said to me, 'Merse, I thought something was wrong, because that injury shouldn't have swollen up like that. It happens to someone when they're taking drugs.'

It wasn't the first time a medic had seen the warning signs. A few weeks earlier I'd broken my nose when we'd played at Leeds. I had to have a plaster cast stuck to the middle of my face – I looked a right wally, but it didn't stop me going out and having a heavy one. The next day I went back to the hospital to have the cast removed, and when the doctor looked up my nostrils he did a double take. I could tell by the look on his face that he knew what I'd been up to. I knew he was thinking, 'This guy's an England international. What the fuck's going on here?'

I could feel the walls closing in on me, which only added to the depression, and that only added to my need to take drugs. It was an ever decreasing circle, and I couldn't see any way out. I was lying to everybody to keep my habit going, covering up my tracks again and again and again. I stopped going out with the lads from the team entirely, because I didn't want them to know, and if ever someone like Bouldy made a suggestion of a double date with the wives, I always swerved out of it. I didn't need that grief. At weekends, I would tell Lorraine that I was on a team do after the game, and I'd tell the lads I was with Lorraine. The truth was, I was in The Mousetrap.

The players never really got an idea what was happening, because that's not the way footballers were together – we weren't that close. At Arsenal, we were matey when we were out, or playing together at the club, but we weren't hanging around all the time. There was the Tuesday Club, yeah, but I had my mates away from Highbury and the lads had theirs, we weren't in each other's pockets all the time. If we were out as a team, we would stick together, but it wasn't like I was ringing up Bouldy or Wrighty at night, wanting a gossip about what was happening at the club, or who had broken up with who in *Home and Away*.

Really, all footballers are like ships that pass in the night. There's an image among the fans that we were all pally off the pitch at Arsenal, but that's not the case at all. Players passed at football clubs, but outside of that there was no other contact really, and we didn't stay in touch after we left Highbury. That's the thing people notice the minute they pack up the game: away from the training ground, there's no one to talk to, and the phone doesn't ring when you've got no one to play for on a Saturday afternoon. It can be very lonely.

Playing for Arsenal, Villa, Boro or whoever was no different from working in an office or doing a shift at a factory. It was a job for most of us, but one that we loved doing. Some people get on at work, some people don't; some people hate one another, others have a group of work colleagues they go drinking with in the week, like I did. It wasn't important for us to be great mates off the pitch, as long as we all clicked on it. When I relaxed, I often liked to do it away from my work-mates, like a lot of people, and that made it easier to slip away unnoticed, especially if I wanted to go off and get wasted with my drug buddies.

Lorraine never worked out I was doing drugs either. It wouldn't have crossed her mind. She'd never been around them or known people who had used them before, so she wouldn't have been able to spot the signs. Lorraine knew that something was going on, but she didn't have a clue it was cocaine. Why would she? It just wasn't something she'd have been knowledgeable on, plus I wasn't around a lot at that time. I was disappearing on two-day benders – going out all night, going to training in the morning, and then going out again – so she hardly saw me. If ever my sons started doing it in years to come, I'd know straight away because I'd recognise the signs. Back then, Lorraine didn't have a clue.

The only thing she might have clocked was the huge amount of time and dough I was spending with the book-ies. The drugs sent me off my head, I was chucking big money away on crazy bets and soon started racking up huge debts – well, even bigger ones than normal.

Do Not Get So Paranoid . . .

Everything was on credit, the bookies knew me and they knew what I did for a living, so they had no problem forwarding me the cash. The problem was, I was spending it quicker than I was earning it and it never felt like real money. It was that Monopoly feeling again. The biggest issue was that I was so high most of the time, I didn't have a clue who or what I was gambling on.

£10,000 on the Eurovision song contest.

£5,000 on bowls match on BBC 2.

£20,000 on an NFL game.

God knows how many thousands on horses and dogs.

I did it all. I was out of my mind.

On the rare occasions that I did spend time with Lorraine or our friends, I'd leave the dinner table halfway through to flick on the Teletext in the other room, so I could check how the St Louis Cardinals had got on or whether bowls star Tony Allcock had won another World Indoor Singles Championship. If we'd booked a restaurant with friends, I wouldn't think twice about excusing myself and checking in with the bookies at the nearest payphone. I was the worst dinner guest in the history of bad dinner guests. It used to drive the missus nuts. She thought I was being rude. I knew I was going off my head.

My problems came to a head in a two-week spell in November 1994. I was a mess, I was doing lorryloads of gear and it was properly messing me up. I went to The Mousetrap on a Saturday night and couldn't stay out of the toilet. I was doing line after line after line. As I stood at the bar, chatting the hind legs off a donkey, my chest started to tighten. My ticker was bang, bang, banging away and I could hardly breathe. I clutched my heart and staggered into the car park, desperately trying to catch my breath. As I dropped to my knees on the pavement, I thought, 'Shit, this is it. My number's up.'

I managed to pull myself together and get myself home, but when we played Brondby in the second round of the UEFA Cup Winners' Cup at Highbury a few weeks later, I was just as bad. I was having my usual paranoia attacks about people catching me out, but after 20 minutes my heart was bursting out of my body again and my lungs felt like somebody was giving me a bear hug. I couldn't run. I honestly thought I was going to drop dead on the pitch. I'd pushed myself to the limit.

That night, on my way home, I even considered killing myself. At one point a lorry was heading towards me and I knew I could end it all if I swerved into its path, but I couldn't bring myself to do it. When I got back to the house, I started undressing for bed, but my mind was a mess. I desperately wanted to guzzle up more cocaine, but I didn't want to die. I dropped to my knees, stark bollock naked in the corner of the bedroom. I started crying, begging out loud for help, shouting for someone to rescue me, but Lorraine was away and there was no one around to hear the yelling. I couldn't see any way out.

Do Not Get So Paranoid...

I'd done so much cocaine that it was impossible for me to get away from the addiction on my own. I knew I was staring death in the face and I didn't have the strength to save myself.

I drove into Highbury the next morning and saw Ken Friar, one of the club directors. I got him in his office. It was confession time.

'I'm struggling here,' I said. 'I need help. I owe thousands and thousands of pounds in gambling debts. I'm in serious trouble.'

Ken looked shocked, and I hadn't even dropped the mother of all bombs yet.

'And I'm addicted to drugs,' I whispered. 'Cocaine.'

I was the biggest football scandal of the decade, maybe the century, and Arsenal were now slap bang in the middle of it. Ken was blown away, but fair play to him, he kept calm.

'Right,' he said. 'We're going to sort you out. We're going to get you help.'

The club called in the FA and their press officer, who was former TalkSport presenter Mike Parry at the time. Mike reckoned I should get into rehab and talk to one of the papers as quickly as possible – that way I could get my side of the story across. I ran an exclusive story in the *Daily Mirror* and then took Lorraine to Paris, so I could tell her the story before it hit the newsstands the next day. When George heard the news he was nothing but supportive.

'Try and keep your wife,' he said, 'and save your marriage – that's the most important thing.'

I couldn't say a bad word about the bloke or the way he handled me. He was right, too, I had some serious explaining to do to Lorraine. George was a nice bloke, he loved me and he knew my uncle very well, so he would often talk to Lorraine as well. He'd already spoken to her about me, because she knew I was in trouble.

'He ain't well,' she said. 'There's something wrong with him.'

They both had an idea I was messed up maybe on booze or betting, but never in a million years did she suspect I'd been doing cocaine. It was a total shock to them both. To be fair to them, there wasn't one person in the world who didn't double-take when they saw the news. It was a massive story, and no one saw it coming. Drugs in football wasn't something that had really happened before, not in the way I'd been doing it anyway. There were reports that Diego Maradona and Claudio Cannigia had been caught out on the gear – Cannigia had been banned for 13 months – but that seemed different, as they'd been spotted with a drugs test. My problem was unique. I certainly didn't know of anyone else in English football doing it. When I was on coke, I didn't hear of one other player with the same interests as me, and I would have known, believe me, because I was on that scene and people talked.

The FA weren't happy. When I told them how much cocaine I was actually taking they went off their rocker. They wanted me to tell the papers I'd only spent £2,000 on it, though it was a bit more than that. They said that if I came out with the truth they'd have to ban me for life, because nobody would accept me coming back into football after doing that much cocaine. It wouldn't have been right. In the end they gave me a ban that amounted to around 20 games, but there were conditions: I had to go straight into a rehab centre where my problems would be looked at. Then I would go through a programme of treatment. I would also have to take all manner of drugs tests for a probation period of 18 months after I started playing again, and I'd have to pay the full cost of the rehab treatment. It all seemed fair enough to me.

Before I could get well there was a press conference to sit through, which was my biggest nightmare. Flashbulbs started popping and people fired questions at me as I started to cry; it was even being shown live on Sky Sports. As the news of my crazy drug binge was played around the world, I bet there wasn't one producer at the station who could even have imagined that I would one day become one of their employees on *Soccer Saturday*. Not in their worst nightmares.

How Not To Be a Professional Footballer

In a prepared statement I told everyone what had happened and explained what a mess I'd made of my life. It was messy. George sat on one side of me, Gordon Taylor of the Professional Footballers' Association on the other. George squeezed my knee for reassurance as I talked; it was his way of showing support, and mate, did I need it. Several times afterwards I asked him why he never put me on the transfer list, and he'd always say the same thing.

'If you own a Robin Reliant and it breaks down, you get rid of it. If you own a Rolls-Royce and it breaks down, you get it repaired.'

I was his Rolls-Royce and needed the occasional trip to the garage, which was a big, big compliment. The only problem was, it wasn't the engine that was playing up, I was filling it with the wrong kinds of petrol. I was now going through a very public MoT.

I explained to the press that I was on a merry-go-round where I'd come home from training and I'd start gambling. The more I lost, the more I drank to drown my sorrows. The more I drank, the more I took drugs. It was Ground-hog Day, every single day. Every day, without fail, I'd gamble, drink, take drugs. Gambledrinkdrugs. I gambled for the buzz; then, when the buzz was gone, I'd drink; then I'd want to keep on drinking; then I'd take drugs. The next day I'd wake up depressed. I wanted to get out of the way I was, but I wanted to have another bet. That was how it was the whole time.

Do Not Get So Paranoid ...

The FA didn't mess about. The minute I finished saying my piece, there was a car waiting to drive me to March-wood Priory Hospital, a rehab centre in Southampton. Everything was happening double quick – I couldn't get my head round it. I think I was in a state of shock during the car journey, as I tried to figure out how I was going to get out of the mess I'd made for myself. When I walked into the hospital, it dawned on me that I wasn't a profes-sional footballer any more, I was a patient just like every-body else in there: the crackheads, alcoholics and heroin addicts. It was them, not the likes of Wrighty, Spunky or Tone, who were my equals now.

I was introduced to a bloke called Dr Tate, who was going to be looking after me during my treatment. He told me it was unlikely I'd be allowed home for Christmas. I was gutted. Even though I was hooked on coke, booze and gambling, there was still a massive part of me that loved my family. I wanted to spend Christmas with Lorraine and my son. Lorraine was also pregnant with our second kid, so I knew it was going to be tough for her with me being away for so long. It broke my heart.

'Forget it,' I said. 'If I can't go home for Christmas, I'm not going in at all.'

A representative from the FA had come with me as I checked in. They wanted to make sure that I stuck to my part of the bargain. He said, 'If you don't go in today, you don't play football ever again. Simple as that.'

'I'm not missing Christmas, mate,' I said. I loved Christmas.

'Well you don't play football ever again.'

Dr Tate then laid it out on the table for me. 'If you miss one Christmas, then you can enjoy loads of Christmases for the rest of your life,' he said. 'But if you're not in here this Christmas, I'll be surprised if you make the next one. You'll probably be dead.'

That scared the shit out of me. I folded. I was missing out on a stack of mince pies and turkey sarnies and heading into treatment, but I knew it was the only chance I had of saving my own skin.

LESSON 10

Do Not Ask for a Potato Peeler in Rehab

'One small step for Merse, a giant leap for sobriety.'

Anyone wanting to know what happened to me, day by day, blow by blow, during those two months in rehab can forget it, because I have. I can just about remember going into Marchwood and coming out again. That's it. Everything else is a blur of meetings, tears and confessions. I honestly can't recall what really happened, not clearly. All I can see is flashes, like a blurry action replay or scenes from an old film. Maybe I can't remember it because it's double hard to go through it again, but instead of skipping over my time in rehab I'm going to tell you, as best as I can, what I do remember.

How Not To Be a Professional Footballer

It might be a bit sketchy, that's all.

The first night in Marchwood, I bawled my eyes out like a baby as I went to sleep. I thought I'd screwed my life up for ever. My room was like a shoe box. Everything was nailed to the floor, because the doctors didn't want patients chucking things around if they'd been upset in a meeting, and so that if they were freaking out at being in the hospital they couldn't wreck the joint. For the first time in ages, though, I was eating properly again. Getting three meals a day just wasn't a priority for me when I'd been bang on the drugs. I used to eat very little. After a week or two of rehab, I was gagging for an Indian takeaway.

I had more meetings than Alan Sugar. Meetings with the police about my drugging (I eventually got a caution, but I was bricking it because I thought it might be loads worse), meetings with Alcoholics Anonymous, Narcotics Anonymous and Gamblers Anonymous. In AA, I learnt that I was an alcoholic because I couldn't predict my behaviour when I had a drink. I'd start boozing and often I wouldn't stop knocking back the beers until I'd passed out. I never knew how I was going to act. In NA I realised I only started doing drugs because I'd got drunk.

Do Not Ask for a Potato Peeler in Rehab

In GA, I learnt that I couldn't gamble responsibly because I have a compulsive personality. That means I go out of control very easily and once I become addicted to something, like telephone gambling, I can't stop myself from doing it. That's why I was totally helpless when it came to betting. I'd bet, and if I won, I wanted to bet again. If I lost, my attitude was, 'Don't worry, mate. You'll make it up with the next bet.' Then I'd bet even harder. I was all over the shop.

When I moved in, the doctors wouldn't let me peel my own apples. I remember going to the canteen one day for lunch and asking one of the counsellors for a sharp knife so I could peel a portion of fruit. She wouldn't get one for me. Instead she took the apple off me and went to the kitchen, then brought it back having peeled it herself. It gave me the right hump – I felt like a little kid – but then I put two and two together and realised it was for the safety of the other patients. *I* knew I didn't want to cut myself or anyone else, but I suppose the counsellors couldn't be so sure that everyone else in Marchwood felt the same.

We had a TV room, but it was weird, because everyone stared at the telly and smoked cigarettes. If there had been a little box of small pens lying around it would have looked like a bloody betting shop.

I learnt that there's no simple explanation for where my problems come from, they're just there. Some people think it's hereditary, like other illnesses; some people think it's to do with what you've experienced in your life from an early age. Other experts make out it's down to luck. I haven't got a clue. The important thing isn't where it comes from. The only important thing is learning how to deal with it.

I knew I would have to change my life for ever when I left Marchwood, and the only way I was going to be cured was to tackle my issues one day at a time, which is a cliché, I know, but it's only a cliché because it was true. I'd have to rely on AA, GA and NA meetings for support to stop the cravings once I got out, which was a nightmare, but it was the only way forward. I learnt pretty quickly that there were no easy cures for my illness.

A week after I entered the Marchwood Clinic, Arsenal fans sang 'There's only one Paul Merson' during the match at Highbury. My dad called me up to tell me. I couldn't believe it. I loved them for it.

Do Not Ask for a Potato Peeler in Rehab

I had to read my entire life story to a group of fellow addicts. They called that stage of the healing process 'Step One', and I had to write out everything that had happened to me in my life. It took me ages, and when I came to reading it out, my story lasted for 45 minutes. I was knackered afterwards.

I remember reading, 'My assets at this time of my life are that if I'm not drunk, gambling or using, I'm a good dad and a lot of people have told me that. I know as well that I am a very kind person. I love buying Lorraine and the kids presents.'

When I first went into Marchwood, I didn't want to tell anybody anything about myself because I didn't trust them. It didn't take long for me to want to tell them everything.

I knew that to stop myself from taking drugs again, I'd first have to stop the boozing and gambling. I only ever really took coke when I was drunk.

I honestly thought I'd be able to keep fit, so I could be ready for training once I'd got back to Arsenal. I tried running every day. One day I met a couple of ladies who were hanging around the courtyard, having a ciggie. I think they were being treated for alcoholism. When I told

them I was off for a run, they said they were up for joining me, but when they went to get changed, the alarm
bells started ringing. One of them came back with her
handbag, the other was in a fancy pair of shoes. After
jogging for two minutes they were both knackered. The
thought of George's first session back at the North Bank,
doing piggybacks up and down the steps, entered
my mind.

'Oh, fuck it,' I said. 'Let's nip into the village and get
some cakes.'

I stuffed my face all the way home.

'Paul, you can go home today.' The best words I'd heard in
months. It was 13 January 1995.

When I left Marchwood, I realised that Arsenal had been
a godsend. They probably should have thrown me out of
the club for ever, but they didn't. When I first came out of
treatment, I still wasn't allowed to play, but that was the
FA's ban, not the club's. They wanted me to miss around
20 games, and they kept pushing the date back and back,
even though I'd missed a lorryload of games while I was
in Marchwood. My counsellor was going spare. He kept
saying, 'He has to play soon or what chance has he got of
making a recovery?'

Do Not Ask for a Potato Peeler in Rehab

I played my first game against AC Milan at home on Wednesday 1 February. I was a sub, but the reception for me when I was warming up was unbelievable. As I ran across the pitch to the other side to play on the wing, Paolo Maldini patted me on the back.

'Welcome back,' he said.

I thought, 'My God, that's massive.'

It dawned on me how big my fall from grace had been. It was huge. No footballer had really been done for drugs like me before, and certainly no one had come back to play top-flight football again. I'd made it back into the first team after going through hell.

Maldini's welcome brought a lump to my throat, no question.

I felt like I'd turned the corner.

Do Not Miss a Penalty in the UEFA Cup Winners' Cup Semi-Final

'Spunky Seaman saves the life of our midfield maestro.'

The thing I craved more than anything after being released from rehab was stability. And not just for me. The last thing Arsenal needed was another scandal coming out of Highbury. I never thought George would be the one to screw it up – but he did, in February 1995, a few weeks after I left Marchwood, by getting done for taking a £400,000 bung from a Norwegian agent called Rune Hauge.

It had happened during the transfer deals for John Jensen and a fella called Pal Lydersen. The club was splashed all over the front pages of the papers again and

Do Not Miss a Penalty . . .

George was kicked out on his arse. I mean, just how stupid can you get? 'Bung, bung, you're dead,' wrote the *Sun*, but honest to God I never saw it coming. None of the lads did. I was gutted, devastated, but not everyone was. I could tell some of the other players didn't like George, because he gave us hell on the training ground and worked us like dogs in games. I wasn't like that, I didn't have a bad word to say about the bloke. He gave me my debut and helped us to win two League titles, a League Cup (he won two of those with Arsenal in the end), an FA Cup and the UEFA Cup Winners' Cup. When my world came crashing down months earlier, he looked after me and helped me through. I was Son of George, and as far as I was concerned he was as good as gold.

I think a lot of the players had the hump with George over the money situation at Arsenal. I could understand their frustrations in a way, because he did treat the club's cash like it was his own. I swear he used to think he was opening his own wallet when it came to dishing out the wages. Players at much smaller clubs than Arsenal were getting better money than us. The board kept a tight hold of the purse-strings, I'm sure, but it was still a mystery to us players why we were under-paid.

I would go in for a contract meeting with him, expecting a good raise because I'd been playing well. I'd sit down, then George would say, 'Right, I'm offering you what'sname pounds. Take it or leave it.'

How Not To Be a Professional Footballer

It was always a shitty offer, but that was it. There was no room for negotiation. If I signed, fine. If I didn't take it, I wouldn't be playing until I did, and that would mean no appearance money and no win bonuses. He had me over a barrel.

Still, I was choked up when he went. I was scared about my future and what would happen to me without him at the club. At the time of his sacking, I was still keeping my rehab diary. When it came to writing this book I flicked through it and noticed I'd described what a bad day it had been for me – one of the biggest setbacks since I'd been out of treatment. I'd written about my initial worries of how the man who had supported me through thick and thin wouldn't be there for me any more, how I was going to miss him and that maybe the new manager wouldn't understand my problems.

The weirdest thing about his sacking and the scandal with Rune Hauge was that George never said goodbye to the lads. When the story came out, he never told us personally. I watched it happen on the news like everyone else and I couldn't believe what was going on.

The assistant coach, Stewart Houston, came in and took charge for the rest of the season, and even though we won our first game against Forest 1–0, a lot of the lads took their feet off the gas. We'd had such a hard time under George that most of us fancied a bit of a breather. I noticed it straight away, everyone relaxed and the team did whatever we wanted on the football pitch. No disrespect to Stewart, but when we went out and played for him, the effort just wasn't there.

The football was great, though; we were knocking the ball about without a care in the world. We went to Crystal Palace and ripped them apart 3-0 shortly after George was sacked - I even got a goal - but I noticed straight away that there was no desire to defend. Nobody was sprinting back at a million miles per hour to protect the back four if we lost the ball. If I gave away possession, I would just stroll back to position. If I'd have lost the ball under George he would have ripped me apart. Even Diego Maradona lost the ball sometimes. If he'd played under George at Arsenal, he'd have been deaf after a week.

With Stewart, everybody went out and played without earache. It was like being back in the school team again, except this time everyone felt like the captain, because nobody was ever going to get dropped. I could have played as badly as I liked and I knew I wasn't getting subbed, not in a million years.

That was the difference between Arsenal and a lot of teams in the League: the pressure to perform all game, every game was huge, or at least it had been under George. If I'd played badly for Arsenal when he was there, I'd have been out of the team the following week, and I'd then have needed to work really hard in training to get picked again. At a big club like Arsenal I knew I had to perform all the time, no excuses.

It was different at Pompey or Villa, and when I went there later in my career, I knew I was getting a game every week and that gave me the confidence to do what I wanted on the pitch. I could express myself, I could do a flick here, a back-heel there. If it didn't come off, I was still going to get picked for the next game. Not at Arsenal, there was too much pressure. That's the difference between a big club and a smaller one. That's why the top-drawer players are the ones that perform every week for a big club, not the ones that stand out at the mid-table teams or below.

When George left Arsenal, the intensity went with him. Because I wasn't getting screamed at whenever I'd hit the first man at a corner, or tracked back too slowly, I relaxed. We all did. We had it pretty easy, which meant we could enjoy the game. Under Stewart, the football was always good to look at. For me that was good. The last thing I needed was any extra stress.

Despite our attacking play, Arsenal weren't ripping up trees in the League under Stewart. We eventually finished 12th, which was pretty crap for us. The fading of our steely streak had cost us points. On the plus side we were once again doing a job in Europe. Despite my 'mare in the

Do Not Miss a Penalty . . .

Brondby game, we got through 4-3 on aggregate. We drew the first match against Auxerre in the quarter-finals 1-1, but beat them 1-0 at their place to make it 2-1 on aggregate in the end.

I had to be careful after the game in France. Everyone was drinking champagne with the directors in the dressing-room and the beers kept on flying around. The journey home was a nightmare. On the plane, the stewardesses were handing out the bevies, but I sat with Wrighty and sucked on an orange juice. There was no way I was going to slip up on the booze. Later Bouldy asked me if I wanted to drink an alcopop. He genuinely thought that would be OK because it was a fruit-based drink. Some people just don't get it, do they?

In the semis we drew the Italian side, Sampdoria. They were a pretty tasty team and featured a few international players like Roberto Mancini and Atillio Lombardo. It was a right ding-dong tie, and after the second leg at their place in Genoa we drew 5-5 on aggregate and the game had to be settled on penalties. Like I needed that. After four penalties, they had missed two; we'd missed one and I only had to score my spot-kick to put us through. No pressure. Honestly, I thought I'd be writing headlines for the paper boys the next morning: 'Former coke addict scores the winning penalty to put Arsenal into the final.' What a story that was.

Except I missed it. I got the shot away and it hit the target, but the keeper saved it. He'd obviously been reading a different fairy tale. I was gutted, I felt sick and I could feel the walls closing in on me again.

'Oh my God,' I thought. 'I've let my team and the fans down, not to mention the club who have believed in me while I've pieced my life together again.'

I knew we would still win the tie if Spunky saved the next pen, but I was a wreck. The odds were always against the goalie in those situations, and I'd blown our big chance.

As I walked back to the centre circle my life started to unravel. I couldn't hear the crowd roaring; I couldn't see my team-mates as they tried to console me. I was trapped in a bubble of self-doubt, and it was a living hell.

'Oh my God, here we go,' I thought. 'All that hard work for this? What was the fucking point? I got drunk loads, got off my head on drugs and gambled away a fortune, but at least I scored penalties when I was messed up. Now that I'm clean, I'm missing them. How is that right?'

The way I was thinking started to panic me, I honestly thought I might go off the rails as soon as I got back to London – my mind was in a spin. I'd done so well up until that moment. Since rehab I'd been regularly attending Gamblers Anonymous meetings and talking to my sponsor Steve, a friend from rehab. Each recovering addict is supposed to have one, so they can talk through their problems if they ever feel like going back on the booze or drugs again. I'd even managed to go into a pub with Nigel

Do Not Miss a Penalty . . .

Winterburn one day after training and not get paro. When I called up the missus and told her where I was, she wasn't happy, but honest to God I didn't touch a drop. Instead I sipped diet cokes and watched the football news on the telly. It was a million miles away from my old life.

All that good work was now in jeopardy. I could hardly watch as Lombardo stepped up to take his spot-kick. He always seemed pretty cool at set-pieces and I'd have put my house on him to score this one. That shows you what I know, because that day Lombardo fluffed his lines and Spunky clawed the ball away. Talk about being let off the hook.

As the lads raced from the centre circle and jumped on Dave, my life started flashing before my eyes. I knew I'd been lucky. I often wonder how my story would have panned out if we'd not got through to the final that night, especially if I'd been the villain. I would have definitely doubted all the work I'd gone through in rehab to put myself on the straight and narrow. Chances are I'd have gone on an almighty binge and ended up in the gutter. I honestly think Spunky saved my skin.

After the shootout, everyone thought we were nailed on to win the final against the Spanish side, Real Zaragoza, but I wasn't so sure. I'd watched them rip Chelsea apart 3–0 in the first leg of the other semi-final; they absolutely murdered them. I couldn't catch my breath watching the match. I knew right then it would be a hard game, but still everyone was talking us up as big favourites, and they were banging on about the fact that nobody had ever defended the cup before, so it was a big deal.

The game was back at the Parc des Princes in Paris. When we checked into the hotel, we had a few hours to kill before a training session at the stadium. Normally I'd have locked myself away in my hotel, blown a few grand in bets and waxed the dolphin for a bit, but I was a clean-living boy all of a sudden, so I put my feet up before heading out with some of the other lads for a haircut because I wanted to shave my barnet off for the game, God knows why. A few of us went, but I was the last one in the chair and, halfway through the cut, the bloke's clippers conked out. He had to hand-cut the rest of it, and it was taking him ages. I was getting nervy.

'I'm not going to get back in time for training,' I thought. Luckily I arrived just in the nick of time. Oh my God, what a result that George wasn't still in charge. He'd have probably dropped me for the final.

In the end it was a choker of a match. Zaragoza went 1–0 up in the 68th minute before Welsh striker John Hartson scored for us nine minutes later. John was a bruiser and was never afraid of getting hurt when he was throwing himself about in the box. He liked the rough stuff, too. Later, when he moved to West Ham, he got into all sorts of bother because he kicked team-mate Eyal Berkovic in the bonce after a nasty tackle in a practice match. I was glad he was playing for Arsenal rather than against us. I wouldn't have fancied dealing with him at corners.

After John's goal, the game went into extra time, but in the last seconds, just as we were getting ready for another nerve-shredding penalty shootout, their midfielder, the former Spurs player Nayim, hit a shot from the halfway line. It went up and up for 40 yards and when it came down, it dropped behind David Seaman's head and into the back of the net. It was probably the most dramatic cup final goal ever, and because of it we were going home potless. We'd lost 2-1.

Fans might say Nayim was lucky, but he wasn't. He had tried the same shot earlier on in the game, but the ball had bounced wide of the penalty area and rolled off the pitch. It must have been something that had worked out for him in training a few times. People blame Spunky for the goal, but I don't. It was an unbelievable shot. The problem was, it was enough to nick the cup off us, because we didn't even have time to attack them again. Everyone was gutted afterwards, but at least I wasn't suffering alone, as I had been in those moments after my penalty miss against Sampdoria.

For me the sad truth was that I'd already won my final winner's medal at the highest level. I won the Division One title with Pompey in 2003 and got to Wembley a couple of times, but that was it. Not that the idea of that crossed my mind at the time. I'd won the

League twice, the FA Cup, the League Cup, the UEFA Cup Winners' Cup – five trophies in five years – and I thought I was going to win trophy after trophy for the rest of my career.

It just goes to show how hard it is to win a cup or a league title when the hot streak ends. A team only has to draw Man United at Old Trafford or Liverpool at Anfield for another year in the FA Cup to be written off. It only takes a tie against Barcelona in the Champions League to cut short a European run. Players and managers don't win cups, the draw does, especially in the FA Cup. Sometimes teams can get through to the final without playing a Premier League side. Most of it is down to luck. And against Real Zaragoza, ours ran out, big-time.

After Stewart had steered us to mid-table, the board decided to draft in someone with a bit more discipline, especially after the drama of the previous season, most of which was my fault. They called up Bruce Rioch, the manager at Bolton Wanderers. He was as about squeaky clean as you could possibly imagine. Bruce was just the person needed by the Arsenal board.

He managed to get the players onside pretty quickly too, though he did that through our pockets. In the summer, after he'd been appointed, he called all the lads into his office, one by one. He gave all of us more money and improved our contracts, which meant nobody was going to moan about him after that. It was a clever move. Then he went out and signed England midfielder David Platt from Sampdoria for £4.3 million and Dennis Bergkamp from Inter Milan for £7.5 million.

Platty was a brilliant player who'd got a lorryload of caps for England and could carve open chances through the midfield, but oh my God, Dennis was probably the best I'd ever seen in my lifetime. Honestly, he was phenomenal – I wouldn't have thought a professional footballer could be that good. His touch, his awareness of the players around him and his passing were all superb.

The thing is, when he signed for us, he couldn't get a goal for toffee. I think it took him around seven games before he finally got used to the pace of the Premiership and scored his first, which arrived against Southampton. Bruce ended up playing him in the hole behind Wrighty, and after that he never looked back. Dennis became one of the best players the Premier League has ever seen. Although it wasn't obvious in his first season, he eventually transformed the team. For the next 10 years, he lit Arsenal up and the fans loved him for it.

People forget what Bruce did for the club when he was there. Signing Platty and Dennis was typical of how he wanted to run a top-flight team. He liked us to play football and he wanted us to get the ball down and play it whenever we could. I remember one time when we played a practice match in training and Martin Keown was up in the centre of midfield. The ball bounced in front of him, but rather than controlling it, Martin booted it up to Wrighty and Dennis. Bruce blew the whistle and went mental.

'Stop! Stop! What did you do that for?'

'I'm just helping the ball on, Boss,' said Martin.

Now, Martin was one of the best man-to-man markers in the game. If Bruce had said to him, 'Make sure Dennis doesn't score in training,' he'd probably have followed him into the toilets at lunchtime, or popped up in the back seat of his car as he was driving home. He was one of those players. But Bruce wasn't having him booting the ball around, he expected him to play football.

'Helping it on?' he shouted. 'But there was no one near you! You could have got that ball down and played it across midfield. When you can, get that ball down and play it!'

That was his philosophy: he always wanted us to play football. If we were 1–0 down with 10 minutes to play in a League game, he'd still have wanted us to knock the ball around. In those situations the natural reaction for any footballer was to bomb it forward, especially when they were under the cosh from the fans, but Bruce always wanted us to think and carve out opportunities. He'd always come into the dressing-room after games like that with the hump. 'If we'd kept on playing we would have made a chance,' he'd say. It was the same with Arsène Wenger when he took over, as you'll find out later.

The difference between Bruce and Arsène, though, was the physical side of the game. Bruce liked us to put it about a little bit. He loved it if we kicked one another in training. One time, John Hartson left his boot in on Tone during a practice match and Bruce was well pleased.

'Brilliant, John!' he shouted. 'That's brilliant, that!'

All the lads were looking at one another in shock – John had nearly cut our centre-back and captain in half. Sometimes I reckoned Bruce still had his Bolton Wanderers head on. He couldn't work out, for example, why we always arrived at training in different cars. Wrighty came in from Crystal Palace, I lived in St Albans and there was probably an hour and a half of driving between the two houses. When Bruce was at Bolton the entire squad turned up in about four cars because all the players lived on the same estate.

His football philosophy worked, though. Arsenal got up to fifth place in the 1995–96 season, which was respectable, and we were back into the UEFA Cup. The only problem was, Bruce was falling out with some of the players, and he'd had a massive barney with Wrighty, who had the hump because he wasn't playing up front all the time. In some games Bruce even played him on the left wing, and the two were at loggerheads. After a match where Wrighty had missed a lorryload of chances, Bruce was livid. He tore him apart in the dressing-room as the lads watched, gobs open in amazement.

'Wrighty? What happened out there?' he said. 'What are you doing? My old centre-forward John McGinlay would have scored those for me.'

Wrighty went into one. It was understandable. You couldn't compare him to John McGinlay, who played for Bolton and – no offence intended – wasn't all that good. Wrighty was a worldy striker. The only thing those two had in common as footballers was that they both had two legs. The situation turned nuclear.

As Bruce carried on talking to the other lads, Wrighty got up and walked to the showers, shouting, 'John McGinlay? Fuck off!'

Bruce was still trying to hold court, but all we could hear was Wrighty spitting blood. I wasn't surprised. John McGinlay and Ian Wright in the same breath? Don't be silly.

'John fucking McGinlay?' seethed Wrighty. 'John McGinlay? Fuck off. Fuck. Off.'

That was it then. When Wrighty handed in a transfer request shortly afterwards, the board knew they either had to lose the player or lose the manager, and Arsenal definitely didn't want to lose Wrighty. He was a superstar at the club and the fans worshipped the ground he walked on. A manager should have known better than to mess with him, because Ian Wright-Wright-Wright was bigger than the club in those days.

It wasn't just down to Wrighty, though. Bruce was also having problems with Tone, who had gone off the rails after Euro 96. He was hitting the booze big time and had got himself injured; his knee was knackered. He later came out as an alcoholic. I think he was on the piss more than I'd ever been. When he opened up in the press I knew I'd actually helped him to come out with his problems. He'd taken one look at me and thought, 'Well, if he's an alcoholic, then I am. My God, I need to get help too.' It turned his life around, no question.

With Tone AWOL, my problems and Wrighty's rucking, Bruce had his hands full. 'I feel like Marje Proops with you lot,' he moaned in the dressing room after a pre-season game against Ipswich Town. For those of you who don't know who Marje Proops was, she spent her days as the agony aunt in the *Daily Mirror*. Most of the time she was dealing with women who had got pregnant behind their husband's backs, or blokes who were suffering problems in the sack. In comparison, me and Wrighty should have been a walk in the park.

Still it wasn't the best thing to say under the circumstances. Bruce was shown the door in the summer shortly after an argument with the board over transfer funds and

How Not To Be a Professional Footballer

Wrighty got to play up front again. Tone was later backed by Arsenal and allowed to piece his life back together. If you ask me, the club had made the smart move.

LESSON 12

Do Not Leave Arsenal with Your William Hill Head On

'Arsène Wenger arrives at Highbury and brings his sugar cubes with him; the revolution begins. Merse follows his betting slips to the Northeast.'

Vice-chairman David Dein came into the Arsenal training ground in September 1996 and told us about our new gaffer.

'His name's Arsène Wenger,' he said. 'He's previously been in charge at Monaco and for the last few years he's been working in Japan.'

Apparently he was the boss at the Japanese club, Nagoya Grampuszackywhat'sname Eight FC (Well, that's what it sounded like to me) and he'd become friendly with the vice-chairman after watching us play against QPR in

173

How Not To Be a Professional Footballer

1988. We were then told he was one of the best managers in the business and that he'd been recommended by Gérard Houllier, who was the technical director of the French FA at the time. Nobody else had heard of him either. All the lads looked at one another and went, 'Who?'

When Arsène turned up he looked like a science teacher and sounded like Inspector Clouseau from the *Pink Panther* films, it didn't help. In fact, it was difficult to take him seriously at first. Ray Parlour spent the morning he arrived whispering the famous Clouseau line 'It's a berm! It's a berm!' in my ear every time he opened his mouth, but by the time we'd finished our first training session with him, I knew that life at Arsenal would never be the same again. The bloke was a genius.

It all started on the day before his first match, which was away to Blackburn on 12 October. Arsène wanted us to do a warm-up session, but rather than taking us out to a training pitch to work our calves, he had us put on exercise mats in the ballroom at the team hotel. Some of the lads started giggling, Ray was doing his 'berm' voice, but after a few demonstrations of what he wanted us to do, the whole squad was groaning away as we stretched this muscle group and that outer abductor. It was a million miles away from anything we'd done under George, Bruce or Don, or even at international level. The old hamstring lunges were gone and instead we were arching our backs and wiggling our hips like the dancers in a Beyoncé video.

Do Not Leave Arsenal with Your William Hill Head On

It worked, though. Arsène's new techniques started to take effect pretty quickly. After a week or two, everyone noticed they were feeling a lot sharper in training and matches, and I felt a lot more supple, more flexible. I felt fresher after games – all of us did. I honestly reckon Tone, Bouldy and Lee Dixon squeezed three or four years more out of their career than they would have ever dreamt of under Bruce or George because of Arsène's stretching techniques. They kept us fitter.

Later, when some of the lads went off to work with Glenn Hoddle in the new international set-up (Terry Venables had left after Euro 96), the England fitness coaches would take the warm-up sessions, but the Arsenal lads would also work on the stretches that Arsène had taught them. The boys from Man United, Newcastle and Liverpool looked over and laughed, but after a while the rest of the team started copying them because any idiot could see that it was working. Everyone felt supple, and the stretches soon became a part of the daily routine, probably because Glenn had played under Arsène when he was at Monaco and knew that he was a smart coach. It was then I realised why England hadn't won the World Cup in decades. We were years behind everyone else. How many more Arsène Wengers were out there?

Behind the scenes at Highbury, he changed the way we went about our day-to-day lives. All of a sudden, the food at the club canteen was different. Lasagne and heavy pasta dishes disappeared from the serving hatch. Instead we were served greens, grilled fish and steamed rice in small portions; there were bowls of raw vegetables with dips. Broccoli came with everything. Today all the players eat like that, but back then it was unheard of and a lot of the lads hated it. Wrighty was always moaning his head off at lunchtime.

'Bloody hell,' he'd whinge. 'What's with all the greens, Boss?'

Everything was measured. For example, we were only allowed to eat certain amounts of steak in the build-up to a game, and it was always weighed out to the ounce. As we were eating, Arsène would wander between the tables, talking to the players. 'You've got to chew to win,' he'd say. He was constantly banging on about eating slowly, because he knew it could help us to lose any excess weight.

Apparently it takes about 20 minutes for the brain to realise that the stomach is full. That meant that by eating slowly I could stop myself from pigging out when I didn't need to. It also meant the food could digest properly and we'd be getting the benefits of all those nutrients in our crunchy greens. It tasted horrible, but we could see his point.

The biggest shock for some of the lads came when the alcohol disappeared from the players' lounge. Managers were always telling their players to cut out the drinking, but Arsène was one of the first to ban it from his club entirely. He'd realised that the game was changing and that footballers were turning into athletes. Getting sloshed after games or restarting the Tuesday Club wasn't going to help anyone if opposing teams were pinging the ball around us at 1,000mph.

Instead, Arsène got us taking vitamins and eating tablets. Before big games we would sometimes go to a Holiday Inn in Islington, where a sports scientist would turn up with a massive syringe. It was filled with a lorry-load of yellow gunk, and as I rolled up my sleeve and lay back on a couch, he'd stick it into my arm. Nobody ever told me what it was, and I'm not sure what it did, but I could always taste it in my mouth when the needle went in. It was pretty strange stuff, but the injections didn't bother me and I was always first in the queue for them. Anything for a buzz.

There were more shocks. Whenever we walked into training, physio Gary Lewin would be waiting to shove a creatine tablet into our gobs. That was Arsenal all over: we never had to do anything for ourselves, it was all done for us. In our dressing-room before the Blackburn match, Arsène walked around and gave all of us a massive brown tablet minutes before kick-off. It was pure caffeine, the equivalent of 10 Starbucks coffees. My heart started banging away, and over 30 minutes later it was still going. When we went back in at half-time, just as the buzz was wearing off, he walked around again, though this time he gave us all a sugar cube.

'What the fuck's all this?' I thought.

He told us to suck on them slowly, and we all looked at each other. None of us knew what the hell was going on. We were used to having teacups chucked at us, not sweets. When we found out that he'd actually watched us play several times before signing his contract with the club, it all made sense. We would often start the second half of a match quite slowly and could sometimes be a bit lethargic. The cubes were supposed to perk up the sugar levels in our blood and keep us sharp after the break. We won at Blackburn 2-0, but some of the lads weren't so chuffed about the caffeine tablets. Quite a few had to run to the khazi with the shits after the final whistle had blown.

Years later, one of my front teeth fell out while I was yapping my way through a match report on *Soccer Saturday*. Jeff and the lads fell about laughing because I had to spend the rest of the show whistling through a gap in my gnashers. When I went to the dentist and got charged a couple of hundred quid for a new tooth, I seriously thought about sending the bill to Arsenal. I'm sure it was down to those sugar cubes.

Do Not Leave Arsenal with Your William Hill Head On

When it finally came to working with a ball in training, Arsène changed everything. Suddenly we were playing eight versus eight practice matches, but with a twist. Sometimes it was a one-touch game, other times two-touch, but the drills were always played in short, sharp bursts. Everything was on the stopwatch and games were timed to the second. After 20 minutes he'd mix it up and we'd play two-touch for a while, but he'd change the rules of the match so maybe the ball wasn't allowed to go back – he wanted us to push our second touch wide or forward. The sessions were double tricky, and we were never allowed to just kick a ball around. Arsène always wanted us to think.

It turned a few of the lads on to management. There were players in that squad who I'd never have thought would become gaffers. Not in a million years. If you'd have said to me in 1989, smashed out of my face with the Tuesday Club, that Tone would go on to be a manager in Azerbaijan, I'd have thought you were having a laugh. A pundit maybe, but not a gaffer. And Bouldy as coach of Arsenal's Under-18 Academy team? Leave it out, he just wasn't one of those lads. The fact that he stopped the messing about and got his manager's head on was all down to Arsène and his new techniques.

I know that when I later left Arsenal for Middlesbrough, I really missed the training sessions. At Boro it was like going back in time to the 1980s. I remember sulking one morning because assistant manager Viv Anderson tried to get the squad to do a beep test. I'm not being funny, but that was old hat. I used to do them in school, and they felt outdated even then. If you can't remember it, the test was a PE drill where school kids would run from one cone to the next before a beep sounded. The longer the test went on for, the quicker the beeps rang out, so runners would have to speed up between cones. I'd always be sweating buckets by the end of it. When Viv tried to do the beep test with 20-odd Premiership players in 1998, I wasn't that impressed. I went up to see the gaffer, who was Bryan Robson at the time, with the hump.

'Boss, I'm not doing this, it's Mickey Mouse.' I said. 'We never did this with Arsène Wenger.'

He took one look at me and rolled his eyes. 'Oh, go home,' he said.

Robbo knew I was a moaner. The lads at Boro had nick-named me Vic, after Victor Meldrew, the grumpy old geezer from the BBC comedy *One Foot in the Grave*. But I was right, it was prehistoric. And Arsène Wenger was bloody space-age.

People go on about Arsène getting a fair amount of silverware over the last two decades, and they're spot on, but it all started with George. Without him, Arsenal wouldn't have won a tap. Arsène was lucky because he inherited a back four that George had built with plenty of hard work and solid tactics. It was so well schooled that Arsène really didn't have to think about who he was going to pick at the back, because the defence picked itself: Spunky in goal, Tone and Bouldy (or Martin Keown) in the middle, and Nigel and Lee Dixon as full-backs. It wasn't broke when Arsène showed up, so there was no need for him to fix it.

Away from the back four, Arsène had an eye for a ball-playing footballer. He'd already signed Patrick Vieira before his first day in the office, and it became clear pretty early on that he was top class. Apparently Arsène had requested the club get him during his own contractual negotiations, but the talk when Patrick came over was that AC Milan had sold him because he'd been hanging around with George Weah, who was the big player in world football at the time, and there had been a few problems. The pair were involved in a car crash, but it seemed the club wanted Patrick out because for some reason they saw him as a bad influence. Anyway, after three months of playing with Arsenal, he was so good that Milan wanted him back for a shedload more cash than they'd sold him for. Arsène had him bossing midfields all over the Premier League.

Nicolas Anelka, his other signing a few months later, was so good it was scary. I honestly thought he was going to be the next Ronaldo (the Brazilian one, not the

Portuguese Fancy Dan), because he was that sharp. You only had to give him a sniff of goal and the ball was in the back of the net. Later, Arsène would sign the likes of Marc Overmars, Manu Petit, Thierry Henry, Sylvain Wiltord and Robert Pires. All of them were top-drawer players.

It wasn't just his transfer policy that impressed me. Arsène also managed to improve the lads who were already at the club, like Ray Parlour. Ray was an honest, hard-working bloke, but nothing out of the ordinary. Arsène turned him into a brilliant midfielder, one of the best in his position in the League, but he was also one of the unluckiest lads in the Premiership because he should have played a load of games for England. Ray's biggest mistake was giving Glenn Hoddle the hump when he took over from Terry Venables (I'll tell you about that one later), but if I'm being honest, I never thought Ray would be as good as he eventually turned out to be.

The thing that impressed me about Arsène was that he wasn't chucking cheques away on average players, all his signings were top class and he always paid sensible dollar for them. Patrick signed for £3.5 million, Nicolas Anelka was only half a million quid. A season later, both those players helped him to win the double for the second time in Arsenal's history in 1998, alongside Giles Grimandi, Wrighty, the old back four and Manu Petit. It was a fairy tale, if you read it in a book you wouldn't believe it. These days, managers believe they have to spend hundreds of millions to win the Premier League, but Arsène was spending next to nothing.

Contrast him with José Mourinho: everyone goes on about how great he is, but everywhere he's been since Porto he's had about a zillion quid to spend on players. At Chelsea, Inter and Real Madrid he's been allowed to buy and sell whoever he wants; all of those clubs are about £185 million in debt afterwards. Arsène would win every trophy in the game if he was to spend money that way, no question, but he'd put the club in a horrible position, and that isn't his style. He thinks like a manager, a chairman, a coach and a fan. Not a lot of managers do.

When I moved to Aston Villa in 1998, the manager, John Gregory went on a bit of a spending spree and bought the likes of Steve Watson for £4 million, Alan Thompson for £4.5 million and Dion Dublin for £5.75 million.

'Crikey, Boss, spending some money, aren't you?' I remember saying to him.

'Well, I might as well,' he replied. 'If I don't spend it, the next bloke in will.'

I suppose, when you look at it that way, it's a fair attitude, but Arsène doesn't think like that, his view is more long term. All right, he might not have won as much as he would have liked in recent years, but it's not like the club are struggling. Still, people say to me, 'How long will it be before Arsenal let him go?' I'll tell you what, if Arsène walked out of the Emirates tomorrow, well, I don't know how many professional sides there are in world football, but all of them would want to have him running their club.

I played nearly every game for him that 1996-97 season. I did miss a few games after having a hernia operation, and Arsène made sure my recovery was fast, if unconventional. He sent me to an acupuncturist after seeing the surgeon. When I went in there, this bloke started sticking pins into the scar tissue and the wound healed so quickly I was back training in next to no time. Within three weeks I was playing for the first team again.

It was phenomenal. When we'd suffered a minor knock and weren't badly injured, Arsène would still get us to see an alternative therapist. If ever I had a bad knee or a sore ankle, he would call in a healer, who would touch my pressure points for half an hour. This bloke would touch something in my gum or squeeze my elbow in a certain way, and when I stood up, the pain was always gone. I don't know whether it was mind over matter, but it worked for me.

If Arsène had a weakness it was his reading of the game. After my hernia op I watched us from the sidelines for a while, and I noticed that he wouldn't change the shape of the side if things weren't working out. He almost always swapped like for like, seldom changing the team around for tactical reasons. His philosophy was to attack and play good football, and he never wanted us to do anything differently.

Arsène didn't do angry team talks either. He never ranted or raved at the players when we were playing badly. I remember we lost 1–0 to Wimbledon at home. When the lads came back into the dressing-room, we all sat there in silence. It was weird. Nobody said a word. If George had been in charge, we'd have been torn apart. Teacups would have been thrown; each of us would have got a hammering. It would have been awful. This time, Arsène just sat there. Then Tone piped up.

'So come on, Boss, what are you going to say? We've just lost one-nil to Wimbledon.'

He shrugged his shoulders. 'What can I say? Ewe just lost to Wimbledon, wern-nil. What do ewe want me to say?'

That was him all over, he'd told us we'd see him in recovery the next day and that was the closest he ever got to losing it. There was no shouting or going mad. I sat there and thought, 'He's right. It doesn't matter how much the manager screams and shouts, we've just been beaten and it's too late to change it now.'

Arsenal went to the top of the League briefly when he first started, but eventually we had to settle for third place behind Newcastle on goal difference. United won the title by seven points, but that didn't matter. Arsène had his eye in for the following season.

When I heard that Bryan Robson wanted to sign me for Middlesbrough in 1997, I thought, 'Bloody hell, that's some compliment.' Robbo was a legend in football, and I mean that seriously because it's a term that gets chucked at some very average players and gaffers these days. When he played for United and England he seemed unstoppable, well, unless he broke something, like an arm or shoulder blade, which he seemed to do quite a lot. But in my head he was a proper star. I wanted to ring my dad so I could tell him, 'Bloody hell, Bryan Robson thinks I'm a player.' I couldn't believe it.

Once I'd got over the shock and heard the wages on offer, I actually wanted to go. The figures were amazing. Middlesbrough had just been relegated from the Premiership, and some big-name foreign players like the Brazilian midfield wizard Juninho were on the first plane home. I was supposed to be his replacement.

Because Boro were a big club, they still could afford to splash £5 million on me, which made me the most expensive signing for a club outside the top flight. They also offered to double the wages Arsenal were paying me. At the Riverside I'd be getting a cool £1 million a year. At the time, I'd started gambling again, but in smaller amounts than I had a few years previously. All I could think was, 'That's a hell of a lot of bets.' I admit it, I was turned by the money even though it felt like Arsenal were on the verge of something big. Everyone else wanted me to stay at Highbury, and when I told Lorraine, she wasn't happy.

Do Not Leave Arsenal with Your William Hill Head On

'What do you want to go there for?' she said. 'We're Londoners. The kids are happy at school. Boro aren't in the Premiership any more. You've got it really good at Arsenal, you won't get anything better.' She was right, but I had pound signs flashing in front of my eyes at the time.

Arsène didn't like the idea of me leaving either. 'I don't want you to go,' he said. 'Where am I going to get a player of your calibre for £5 million? But Merse, I also understand that they are offering you a lot of money, so I won't stand in your way if you want to sign for them.'

He offered to up my wages to £635,000 a year, in a four-year contract, which was a lot of money, but I reckoned I could have got more. I knew Dennis Bergkamp was probably getting a higher wage than me, but then I wasn't Dennis Bergkamp.

'We have a wage structure here,' Arsène said, when I pushed him on the cash. 'I don't want to break it.'

That was that: I could tell that Arsène was a manager who didn't want his players thinking about money. If you did the business for him, the money would come, but I wasn't that patient and I turned his offer down. He must have thought, 'Wait a minute, I've offered him this deal, and it's good money and he's not taking it? Let him go ...'

I just couldn't turn my back on the telephone number cheques that Bryan Robson was offering me, and the fact that Arsenal couldn't up the wages was doing my head in a little bit. I didn't understand how a club like Arsenal couldn't match what I was being offered by Middlesbrough – a much smaller club who'd just been relegated. Arsenal were one of the biggest clubs in Europe, and a club I'd been for at 14 years. I would have stayed if they had offered me more dough. Sure, the Bryan Robson factor was a part of getting me to Boro, but now I'm older, I've realised I moved for the money. I was being greedy.

Later that day, I signed with Boro. I walked out of Highbury for the last time as an Arsenal player, but it wasn't the emotional experience I'd imagined it to be, I just packed my stuff and went. There was no leaving party, no cards, and definitely no champagne. Like I said earlier, footballers are like ships passing in the night, and I was heading elsewhere. It was only a little while later that I really appreciated what a special place Arsenal was and that I was letting my betting slips rule my heart.

I went home to the wife and said, 'I've got a four-year contract with Boro.'

She wasn't happy. 'I'm not moving,' she said.

I couldn't believe it. 'Why not?'

'I told you before, the kids are settled and I don't want to move up north. I wasn't joking.'

Then I felt gutted. I'd just signed a massive contract and doubled my wages, but instead of celebrating, I was about to move to the Northeast and Division One football on my Jack. Lorraine was right: I'd never had it so good as I had at Highbury.

Do Not Let Gazza Move into Your House

'Merse's life in a Middlesbrough mansion with football's favourite boozehound, Paul Gascoigne. What could possibly go wrong?'

Robbo was so laid-back as a gaffer, it was ridiculous sometimes. In my first game for Boro, a friendly, the lads came into the dressing-room at half-time and the boss started dishing out instructions. All of a sudden, Gianluca Festa, our Italian defender, reached into his suit pocket and pulled out a phone which had been ringing away for hours. I couldn't believe it, he actually had the neck to answer. Festa mumbled something quickly in Italian and then hung up. I sat there with my mouth open in shock.

That would never have happened at Arsenal. George or Arsène, even Bruce Rioch would have thrown Festa out just for having a phone switched on in the dressing-room. Had he done that while any of them were giving a team talk, he'd have been dropped for a decade. Robbo wasn't bothered, but that was the difference between a top, top team and one that wasn't so professional, and you only had to look at the League tables in the paper to see who was doing it right and who wasn't. Arsenal were building a double-winning team; Boro had just been relegated.

It was scary at times how unprofessional the club could be. Boro and Arsenal were dog and duck. When I signed for them I hadn't met Robbo, so I was told to get over to Italy, where the first team were having their pre-season training camp. A friendly had also been set up with a local Mickey Mouse side, just to give the players an extra work-out. I got on the first plane out there, but when I landed, nobody was waiting for me. Not a soul. Now, I'd just come from Arsenal where everything was laid out on a plate. If I was meeting Arsène Wenger for the first time like that, I'd have bet my life that a car would have been waiting to pick me up; and a representative from the club would have been on hand to say hello. Not with Boro. I was on my Jack.

I managed to hail a taxi, which then drove me out to the middle of nowhere. The trip lasted five hours and took me down a hundred dusty tracks and all sorts of backroads. I can't imagine how much it must have cost the club in pounds when they sorted out my expenses that month, but I remember having to hand over about eight billion lira in notes to the driver.

The chaos didn't end there. On the first morning, before training started, I knocked on the physio's door. It was about nine o'clock, so not early, but when he answered he eyed me up like I was a piece of crap on the bottom of his shoe.

'Can I have my strappings done, please, mate?'

He went mental. 'What's the time?'

'About nine.'

'Nine? Nine! Come back at half past.'

He slammed the door in my face.

That day, the friendly we were there to play turned out to be a match against the waiters from the hotel. I remember thinking, 'What the fuck is going on here?'

In my first few months at Boro, I was like a fish up a tree. I was useless on the pitch, and off it I felt unsettled. The missus still wasn't having the idea of us moving up to the Northeast as a family, so at first I'd have to drive up to training every day on my own. St Albans to Darlington, a five-hour trip in the dark listening to Crap FM all the way there. Can you imagine sitting in a car for five hours before football training? It killed me. My back was in knots before I'd kicked a ball in anger. Then I'd have to spend five hours driving back after training to get home. I'd hit St Albans just in time for the rush hour.

I was constantly knackered and couldn't get my game going. In my first month at the club I think I only scored one goal, which was against Stockport on a Tuesday night. I was supposed to be the club's Next Big Thing, the player to replace Juninho, but I was having a shocker. Our other big player, Fabrizio Ravanelli, left a few weeks into the start of the season, although I never actually met him. I'd heard that his head was so far up his arse he couldn't actually bring it out to say hello. Don't get me wrong, he was a good player, but in my opinion he was only out for himself.

Because of my poor start to the season, Boro had the hump with me. They were paying a lot of money in wages and I wasn't doing the business. The fans had the hump too. The team hadn't had a great start and we were miles away from the top of the League. Our form was patchy. Although we'd beaten Charlton on the first day of the season and later Tranmere, we'd lost to Stoke and drawn with Stockport and Bradford. It was hardly title-winning form. The crowd were getting on my back a little bit and, to be fair, I couldn't blame them. Robbo called me into his office.

'Merse, you've got to move up,' he said. 'The car journey is affecting your fitness and we need you to be on top of your game.'

Do Not Let Gazza Move into Your House

I told him I couldn't, because my wife and kids weren't going to move and I knew I'd get homesick. I was like that in those days, so the club came up with a Plan B. I had to catch the 7.47 a.m. train from Stevenage – which was a 20-minute drive from my house in St Albans – to Darlington, where there'd be a cab waiting to drive me to the training ground. I'd train for a few hours, and then another taxi would pick me up to take me back to the station for the 2.01 train home. Even if the other lads were still working, or if there was a double training session, I'd be allowed to go early. The club picked up all my travel receipts.

Another month passed, but still my back was done in. Sitting on a train for a few hours wasn't much of an improvement on the long car journey, and my form hadn't exactly set the world alight the way the fans and board had hoped. Robbo called me into his office again and put his foot down.

'Merse, you've got to move up,' he said. 'You're still not flying in the League and we need you to be fully fit, so you can't commute any more. We've given it a go and it's not working. Fabrizio Ravanelli's old place is available. It's a six-bedroom mansion in Hutton Rudby – you can move in there.'

I told him I wasn't having it and came out with the same old excuse. 'My wife and kids are down south, blah, blah, blah …', but I could tell he was sick of hearing it. Robbo then told me that by refusing to move up I was in breach of contract. Boro could sue me if I didn't do as I was told. I shut up and packed my bags, I didn't need a legal issue hanging over my head, but I really couldn't handle knocking around a big old mansion on my own all week. I was really worried that too much idle time alone might cause some personal issues with the drinking, gambling, or worse.

Robbo knew too. 'Do you know of anyone who might move up with you?' he said.

I figured my brother Keith could drop tools and live with me. He was a van driver in London.

'Get him up to The Riverside next week,' said Robbo. 'We want to talk to him about working here.'

Keith thought the world had gone mad when I told him. He drove up to Middlesbrough in his van and sat in the boardroom. A few minutes later I swear his eyes nearly popped out when Robbo walked into the room and shook his hand. He was so excited to meet a football legend. Then it got even better. Robbo told Keith the club were making him part of the Boro wage bill and his earnings would be £400 a week, pretty unreal for a van driver in 1997. His official role was to sit there and keep me company while I watched the telly in the evenings. That was better news than winning the Lottery, as far as he was concerned. Keith thought he'd died and gone to heaven.

Do Not Let Gazza Move into Your House

I don't know how I came to share a house with Gazza – I can't remember whose idea it was or when it was first suggested – but with three months of the season left we were housemates. We were the original screwed-up couple. Gaz was an alcoholic and a brilliant nutter. I was an alcoholic and a compulsive gambler with a history in class A drugs. It was like a time bomb waiting to go off, but it was a right laugh. Gazza was a great lad to be around. Most of the time it was non-stop laughter.

He had signed for Boro in March 1998 and moved in with me until he found his own place. He'd left Glasgow Rangers because he was desperate to get his England career back on track and the World Cup in France was just around the corner. Boro were willing to spend some money on him, but I doubt that they'd have been as keen if they knew how bad Gaz was caning it. When I travelled up on the 7.47 train one morning after spending some time at home with the family, Gazza met me halfway. He had a bottle of red wine in his kitbag and started knocking it back while the other commuters sipped coffee and scoffed croissants for breakfast. I must have said to him a hundred times, 'Oh Gaz, you cannot do that, mate. Not when we're training and playing. You won't get to the World Cup.' But it didn't stop him from draining the whole bottle.

I also had an outside chance of making the World Cup squad myself, because Glenn Hoddle had recalled me into the international set-up, despite my playing for a lower-league club. After moving up to the Northeast permanently, my form had rocketed. At one stage in the season, the club programme reckoned I'd been involved in setting up 75 per cent of the team's goals. Glenn, as he had proven at club level with Spurs, Monaco and Chelsea, was a footballer's footballer. He wanted skilful players and as my season started to improve, he drew me back into the squad.

I was well pleased. International football was something that I'd been aiming for, to be honest. When I first went into treatment at Marchwood in 1994, I was told by my counsellor that I had to have a goal for when I left the hospital, something much bigger than just getting on with normal, everyday life. I told them my plan was to play for England again.

The counsellor looked at me like I was joking. 'I wouldn't go that high,' he said.

I wasn't having it. 'I will,' I said. 'It's going to happen.'

When Glenn rang up and told me I was back in his plans, it made all the hard work worthwhile.

I loved Gazza, though. He was a bundle of laughs to be around and a lovely, lovely bloke. Honestly, if you were standing at the bus stop in the pissing rain without a penny in your pocket, Gaz would have given you his last tenner for a cab, then he'd walk home himself. That's the type of bloke he was. Gaz's biggest problem was that he was a joker. I don't mean that in a horrible way, but he just was. Something weird or funny was always happening when he was around.

Whenever he was in the house he'd always be stark bollock naked. He'd never wear a stitch. It was a gorgeous gaff too, very grand with big windows and fancy balconies, but when Gazza moved in, I always found him kipping on the sofa first thing in the morning. It dawned on me after a while that he'd been sleeping there all night.

'What are you doing, Gaz?' I asked. 'Why don't you go to bed?'

He looked at me like I was mental. 'There are beds here?'

He'd moved into a six-bedroom house and hadn't even realised. Nobody ever took his spot on his settee, though, not after he'd sat down on it naked having told everyone he'd been for a shit. He had that all to himself.

Gazza would do weird things just to lose weight. He'd take sleeping tablets after training and then go straight to bed when he'd got home in the afternoon. It was the only way he knew of stopping himself from eating. When he woke up again hours later, he'd drop another pill to knock himself out again. It was a dangerous habit.

The problem was, being around Gazza's demons had brought me closer to mine. For the first time in my career

How Not To Be a Professional Footballer

I was feeling the strain. Pressure. Like a weight on my shoulders. I felt it all through my first few months at the club as I left my family behind to move up north, but I kept a grip on it. As the club chased promotion throughout the season, the expectation of getting back into the Premiership became massive too. Even though Arsenal were a big, big team, there was never any stress, probably because I'd come through the ranks. At Boro, the fans saw me as a direct replacement for Juninho and they wanted to win the title. Now that was a nightmare and I couldn't handle it. At the beginning of March, just before Gazza arrived, I handed in a transfer request because I was so unhappy, but the boss knocked me back.

I think he understood my problem, though. Juninho had been the supporters' big hero, which was unsurprising because he was some player. He was a midfield whizz and also Brazilian, which always got the fans' pulses going. I was from St Albans, and it just wasn't the same. From the minute I signed, the heat was on me to perform in every game. By the time Gaz had signed, I'd relapsed. I started to gamble more often because I thought it might take my mind off the promotion charge. At first it was small time: £50 bets in February, £75 ones in March, flutters of £100 in April. Horses were my bet of choice at the time, and I probably blew about £7,000 all told.

When Gaz started drinking at our shared pad, I soon caved in. One Sunday I got back on the booze, but given that I was sharing a house with football's favourite nutter, our session had a crazy twist: we started playing a drinking game that Gaz knew which involved sleeping tablets and red wine. If it sounds suicidal, that's because it was. Gaz would send Jimmy Five Bellies to a fancy hotel to buy the grog. He used to go there himself quite a bit to relax, but he couldn't have bought any booze there without word getting back to the club. Living in Middlesbrough was like living in that Jim Carrey movie, *The Truman Show*. I would see a familiar face in the health club in the morning, then I'd see them at the supermarket in the afternoon. If I went out to a restaurant in the evening, chances are I'd see them there as well. It was a real goldfish bowl existence, and as professional footballers, we couldn't get away with anything.

For the game, Gaz wanted the wine from this one particular hotel because it was nice stuff, but I swear Jimmy was going to the local Spar to get it because it tasted like vinegar. It was my first drink in three and a half years. When Jimmy came back we all started knocking back glass after glass. We'd drink a glass and then take one of Gaz's sleeping tablets; the game was based on stamina. Whoever stayed awake the longest won and scooped up a few grand in bets. We played the game a few times while Gazza was living with me. It's a miracle it didn't kill one of us, but it's all we had to do, because there was nothing else to keep us occupied up there. In

How Not To Be a Professional Footballer

Newcastle you could lose yourself a little bit in the town, because it was so big, but in Boro there was nothing. Apart from football.

Oh my God, Gaz was brilliant at that. I honestly think he was the best English footballer I've ever seen in my life. Whenever he played, he set the place alight. The standard of football wasn't great in the Championship at that time, which was perfect for me because it made me look good, but for someone like Gazza it was important that he had good footballers alongside him for it to work.

I firmly believe that you're only as good as the players around you. People go on about Ryan Giggs and Paul Scholes at United and how they were great at 35. Don't get me wrong, they were great players, but they wouldn't have been playing like that if they weren't at United with the likes of Ronaldo, Tévez and Rooney helping them out.

Teddy Sheringham was a great example of how that theory worked. He was a fantastic footballer, and it didn't matter that he lost pace as he got older because he had a brilliant brain. He fitted in everywhere he played because he was with good footballers, except at Colchester. At Colchester he was finished in about five minutes. It wasn't that he became shit overnight, he was just so far ahead of everyone else that they made him look like a pub player. He was flicking balls around the corner for midfielders to run on to, but they were still on the half-way line picking their noses. When he was at Spurs, Pompey or West Ham there were players living off those clever passes.

Gazza was only 30 at the time, but Robbo had built a good team for him to play in. We had Andy Townsend, who was a blinding footballer, Mark Schwarzer was in goal, and Gianluca Festa had shored up the defence, so there were some good players on show. By the time Gaz arrived at The Riverside we were in our stride and the chase for promotion was between us, Sunderland – where my old mate Niall Quinn and his strike partner Kevin Phillips were scoring goals for fun – Charlton and Forest.

We even got to the League Cup Final against Chelsea. We'd beaten Liverpool over two legs in the semi-final, which was some result because they had a proper team. Jamie Redknapp, Steve McManaman and Michael Owen were in the side. At Anfield we lost 2-1 but I scored one of my best ever Boro goals. Craig Hignett put me in from the halfway line and as I closed in on goal, I looked at putting the ball in one corner past keeper David James and then I knocked it in the other. It looked good on the telly, but it was never meant to happen.

In the return leg, we did them 2-0 at our place which was enough to get us to the final. It wasn't a fluke. You can beat anyone over 90 minutes, but to win a tie over two games was a massive deal. When we got to Wembley, Robbo put Gazza in the squad, even though he'd been at the club all of 10 seconds. Craig Hignett missed out despite all his hard work in getting us there. I could tell he was gutted and that Gazza was embarrassed, but he had no say in the matter. If Robbo had said to him, 'Do you want to play in the final?' he'd have told him no. After we lost to Chelsea 2–0 in extra time, Gazza went up to Higgy and gave him his loser's medal. It was a nice touch, though I'm not so sure what he'd have done if we'd won that day.

Boro's coach, Gordon McQueen, lived next door to Gaz and me in Hutton Rudby. He'd been quite a player in his day, turning out for the Leeds United side of the 1970s before winding up at Man United. He was a big name to work with. When midfielder Andy Townsend signed for the club from Aston Villa, he moved five minutes down the road. People were always popping in and out, but Gaz was out more than most, strolling around the house in his birthday suit.

I used to love living next door to Gordon, he was a right laugh. His wife made a fuss of us and she would always cook dinner for me, Gazza, Andy Townsend and my brother during the week, or on a Sunday if we weren't playing. Sometimes, we'd all be eating and

Do Not Let Gazza Move into Your House

Gordon would get up as soon as he'd finished his last mouthful.

'Right,' he'd say, 'I'm off to the pub.'

Then we would hear the door slamming behind him. He'd always leave us behind. He probably knew what would happen if he invited us along.

I remember a couple of seasons later, I was captain of Villa and we played Boro in the League. Whenever I was skipper, I'd always have to go into the ref's room before kick-off with our coach, the opposition's captain and their coach, who was Gordon that day. The rules stated that both sides had to swap teamsheets, but as the papers were being handed over and everyone began chatting away, Gordon started to shout. His fists were clenched.

'Get in there!' he yelled. 'Get! In! There!'

I looked at him, I didn't have a clue what was going on. 'What's up, Gordon?' I said.

'Oh, I've got Ian Taylor in my dream team.'

Honestly, he was the coach of a massive club like Middlesbrough, but he was more worried about his fantasy football side than his own line-up that afternoon. What a legend.

How Not To Be a Professional Footballer

About a month before the end of the 1997-98 campaign, Robbo called me into his office.

'It looks like we're getting into the play-offs,' he said, 'because we'll need to win all six of our last six games to get automatic promotion.'

On paper he was right. Forest were top and Sunderland were four points clear of us in second place. We'd suffered a bad run of results, and for four or five games we'd looked knackered. A fortnight or so earlier, we'd played a League game against QPR. They were hammering us 5-0 at half-time. Their left-winger, Mark Kennedy, who was on loan from Liverpool, had ripped us to shreds. We were too tired to keep up, and first or second place in the table looked a million miles away.

I thought, 'Here we go, the boss is going to go Radio Rental in the break,' but he was as calm as you like. In those days, the League was based on goals scored rather than goal difference, and at that time in the season it was looking pretty tight, so every goal we got counted. The stakes were high in the points department too, but that day Robbo didn't seem bothered.

'Right,' he said. 'We're losing this one, just get out there in the second half and get as many goals as you can. Even if we lose 10-2, make sure you get two goals.'

It was such a refreshing attitude. He wanted to entertain the fans all the time and score as many goals as he could for them. We still lost 5-0, but it was the thought that counted.

Do Not Let Gazza Move into Your House

After the QPR beating, Robbo wanted me to take a couple of weeks off so I could be recharged for the play-offs, but I wasn't slacking off.

'No, I'm fine, Boss,' I said. 'I want to play, definitely.'

I was right, as well. We went on a run, winning five of our last six games, which turned out to be enough because Sunderland lost to Ipswich on a Tuesday night. That meant we had to beat Oxford on the last day of the season to go up without getting involved in the play-offs. At half-time it was 0-0. After 90 minutes we'd put four past them and were back in the Premiership as Division One runners-up.

That night, I got home just in time to catch *Match of the Day* on the telly. No lie, just as I flicked it on, I saw Tone running through the Everton defence at Highbury. He blasted the ball home, scoring the fourth in a 4-0 win, and it was some goal. It also meant that Arsenal had won the League with two games to spare and I was made up for them. It was a great end to the season. I thought, 'Wow, we've just got promoted and Arsenal have won the title. What a result.'

I didn't look at it with regret. I didn't think, 'Oh, that should have been me doing that,' because I'd made my decision and I couldn't have asked for anything more at Boro. Arsenal would go on and win the FA Cup in a 2-0 victory over Newcastle to secure the double, and I was well chuffed for Arsène, Tone and the rest of the lads.

How Not To Be a Professional Footballer

Even better, there was a World Cup looming in France. A few weeks later, I got word that I'd made it into Glenn Hoddle's provisional 30-man squad for France 98. I was soon packing my bags and heading off on another football jolly.

LESSON
14

Do Not Ask Eileen Drewery for a Short Back and Sides

'Merse heads to France with the Nuggets and Sport Billy; he is touched by The Hand of Hodd. Penalty heartbreak ensues.'

Glenn Hoddle's biggest problem as an international manager was his skill. He was still a better footballer than some of the lads in England's 1998 World Cup squad, and a lot of them didn't like it. One or two called him 'Chocolate' because they reckoned that if he'd been made by Cadbury's he'd have spent the whole day licking himself, but the truth is, they were jealous. Glenn was still a player. If he could have run about a bit more, he'd probably have been good enough to play that year.

I remember one training session in France when David Beckham and Paul Scholes were taking free-kicks,

popping off shots at Spunky in nets. It wasn't really working out for either of them. Balls were flying over or going
a million miles wide, anywhere but on target. Glenn was
watching from the touchlines, and after 10 minutes he'd
had enough.

'Stop!' he shouted.

He placed the ball down and said, 'This is what I want.'

In a heartbeat – dink! – he'd curled the ball past Spunky
and into the top corner. It was different class, the others
couldn't top it.

He was strict too. The messy nights we'd regularly
enjoyed under Graham Taylor stopped because Glenn
wouldn't stand for any drinking. It was only allowed on
special occasions. Because he had worked under Arsène
Wenger at Monaco, he had similar ideas about diet and
nutrition. Booze was definitely off the menu, which was
good news for me and Tone, seeing as we were both
recovering alcoholics. At dinner we were eating broccoli,
steamed fish and pasta, just as Arsène had taught the
Arsenal lads.

Glenn later blew it big-time when he shot his mouth off
in an interview with *The Times* in 1999. He told a journalist
that it was his belief that disabled people were being
punished for the sins they'd committed in a previous life. It
was wrong, and he got slaughtered after that – even Tony
Blair had a pop at him – so it wasn't a surprise to any of the
lads that he got the boot, but I was gutted because I

thought he was a top-drawer gaffer. If he hadn't given that interview, he'd still be managing the England side now.

When he was running the show, Glenn's biggest asset off the pitch was that he was great at keeping the lads relaxed. He was very soothing. I could sit there and talk to him all day about football, health, beliefs, relationships, anything. He was interested in life and other people's stories, and I'd had a more interesting journey than most. Glenn wanted to talk about my experiences, and I was happy to tell him, no problem, because my drug problems were over and done with and a lot of people were interested in it at the time.

A lot of his fascination came from his spiritual side. This caused a bit of a fuss with the fans and the press, because Glenn was a born-again Christian and had brought a faith healer called Eileen Drewery into the England set-up. She'd started talking to the lads during the qualifiers for France 98. Glenn thought she would bring some calm into the squad, which probably wasn't a bad idea with Gazza, Tone and me on board, but the papers went mental over it. They even nicknamed us 'The Hodd Squad', but the truth was, religion, spirituality - call it what you want - it worked on me.

Between Glenn and Eileen, my head was in a good place when I went on England trips. Glenn even made sure the flying was OK. I remember when we went to Casablanca to play World Cup warm-up fixtures against

How Not To Be a Professional Footballer

Morocco and Belgium, I was having a 'mare because the flight over was a horror show. When we came in over the mountains to land at Casablanca I began to panic. The freak-outs started and I could feel my palms getting sticky. Glenn could see I was bricking it and turned round to me as I sat there, gripping the armrests.

'You all right?' he said.

'I hate flying, Boss. I'm shitting myself.'

'Don't worry, Merse. It's going to be OK. We *won't* crash.'

I thought, 'Thank God for that. Glenn's said we're going to be safe. Nothing's going to fuck with us now.'

That's what I was like, and still am: because Glenn had told me we were all going to be OK, I calmed down instantly. It reminded me of a time when I got on a flight a year earlier and started having a panic attack before the plane had even taxied on to the runway. My shirt was soaked through with sweat and I was thinking of doing a runner, but as I was sitting there, Sir Nick Faldo got on to the plane.

'Oh my God,' I thought. 'We're going to be OK. Nick Faldo isn't dying in a plane crash.'

I was fine for the rest of the flight. The way home was another story, though, because Sir Nick was nowhere to be seen. I spent ages looking for him again, fretting because I couldn't find anyone vaguely famous in the seats. I took it as a sign that the plane was going down.

Do Not Ask Eileen Drewery for a Short Back and Sides

When Glenn suggested talking to Eileen Drewery, I was up for it. Some people are open-minded, some aren't; some people believe in religion and spirituality, others don't. I was open-minded. I went to see Eileen and talked to her for ages. We'd always meet in her hotel room and chat openly about my problems, what I'd done in the past and how I was coping with everything. She used to put her hands on my head and talk about spiritualism. Before her, the only spirits I'd ever discussed were the ones behind the bar in the Rose and Crown.

When I sat in her chair, she rubbed my bonce and talked about demons and how they got into my soul whenever I drank booze or took drugs. It scared me sometimes. I used to think, 'Shit, for all the drinking, drugging and gambling I've done, are there loads of demons inside of me already?'

I took it all on board, though, and it helped me to stay straight after my relapse at Boro. Then I'd try anything to help me through the tough times, when I would come close to drinking or betting big again. I wanted to get well. Did it work? Did it not? I don't know, but I knew that if I was open to alternative therapy like the stuff Eileen was doing, then I had a better chance at least. I'd decided to go for it, as did some of the others. I know a few of the lads would go to see her if they had an injury. She'd lay them down, but rather than putting her hands on their head, she'd place them over the hamstring or calf. With me, I could always feel as if I was healing somewhere, but I couldn't really tell where. After her sessions, I always felt as fresh as a daisy.

There were one or two players who took the piss. Apparently when Robbie Fowler met her, he ended up watching the telly with her husband rather than talking to Eileen. Ray Parlour went to see her and it seems he was even less enthusiastic. God knows what really happened, but when he bumped into some of the lads afterwards he was pretty cocky about the meeting. I asked him how he'd got on.

'Yeah, all right,' he said. 'I asked for a short back and sides.' Glenn got to hear about it from Eileen and that was that as far as Ray was concerned. Glenn had very strong beliefs, and Ray was out. He never played for him again, even though he was in the form of his life at Arsenal. In fact, he was playing so well that Arsène Wenger called the FA to find out why Glenn wasn't picking him.

Arsène told them that he thought Ray was the best midfielder in the country at that moment. He asked why he wasn't getting a game. The message came back that Ray simply wasn't in the frame.

England qualified for France 98 as group winners, beating the likes of Moldova, Poland and Georgia along the way. Our only sticky spells came against Italy. They beat

Do Not Ask Eileen Drewery for a Short Back and Sides

us 1-0 at Wembley and we needed a draw in Rome to put us on the plane to the World Cup finals and condemn them to a play-off. We got through with a goalless draw, but in fact we played well enough to have beaten them on their own patch.

Even though I didn't feature in that game, Glenn called me up to his pre-tournament group of 30 players, eventually naming me in his final squad for France. This was a big deal because I was the only player in the squad who hadn't played in the Premiership that season. I'd always figured my chances of making the final 22 were slim, as no one really goes to a World Cup with England if they haven't been playing in the top flight.

Gazza wasn't so lucky. He was booted out of the group at the last minute because he'd been boozing hard and was having a personal meltdown. It all started in the run-up to the tournament when the press spotted him out on the town with radio DJs Danny Baker and Chris Evans. He fell out of a kebab shop and a photographer was on hand to snatch a picture of him looking blotto. The *Mirror* ran it on the front page the next day.

By the time we'd got to our base at La Manga in Spain, where the squad was going to be trimmed to 22, the manager had seen enough. It all kicked off on the weekend that Glenn was due to announce his squad, and the lads were given a break because we'd been working so well. It was a Saturday night, so we were allowed a party with a few beers at the hotel, not that it meant anything to me and Tone. The pair of us wandered around the complex eating sarnies and having the odd cuppa. When we looked into the bar to see what the other players were doing, Gazza was paro. He was sitting at the hotel piano trying to play a tune.

The next day we were allowed a golf competition on the local course before a series of individual meetings with Glenn that started at 4.15. They were being held so he could tell each of us whether we were going to France or not, and the lads were a bag of nerves, but Gazza took it as a sign to get rotten drunk again. He was paro on the golf course as he played with Incey, Spunky and Spurs keeper Ian Walker. When he got back to the hotel, me and Tone tried to sober him up by stripping his clothes off and chucking him into the pool. God knows what the paying guests must have thought as they stared at us.

By the time Gaz went for his meeting, Glenn's mind was made up. He must have looked at him and figured, 'No chance. I can't take him away for six weeks. Is he going to drink like this when we get to France?'

When Gazza was told he going home, he lost it, even smashing a lamp in Glenn's room. His world caved in. It was a real shame, and personally I think he'd got us to the tournament on his own. He played an absolute blinder against Italy in Rome, but like my run-in with Terry Venables in 1994, Gaz had been given enough rope to hang himself. Leaving him out was a big decision, but Glenn wasn't scared of making big decisions. The weird thing was, even though I was in the squad, Glenn's choice worried me. Gazza was a much better player than me, and I couldn't lose the idea that I was only going because he'd been dropped. When I asked the boss, he shook his head.

'No, Merse, you were both going to France,' he said.

Gazza would probably have gone crackers in the World Cup. Being in the finals of an international tournament can be really boring, especially if you're not playing, and before I went I knew I wasn't going to play a lot because I was a utility player. With Boro, and Arsenal before them, I could play up front as well as on both flanks. Being able to perform in a few positions will always get you a lorryload of club games and a lorryload of call-ups, but it won't get you a lorryload of caps. If I'd had one position only, I might have played more for England. Instead I was being called up to squads because I could play in three or four spots and could plug gaps if anyone got injured or suspended.

That meant I wasn't involved in the World Cup games in France too much, I felt a million miles away from home, and I missed Lorraine and the kids. France also felt like such a big place. The teams weren't put together in an Olympic Village-style resort, we weren't in the same town or city as all the other players, so we felt very separate.

How Not To Be a Professional Footballer

The nearest team was a flight away, and the travelling was a big issue. Once the tournament got under way, I found it quite tough, because we were flying across the country for games, staying in hotels and then going to the matches. It reminded me of the FA Cup Final: playing in a World Cup was nowhere near as exciting as watching it on the telly.

Glenn wanted us to concentrate all the time, though. During training he would get the first team to work on set-pieces while the rest of us watched from the side-lines. He was forever saying to us, 'Always be alive, because if you have to come on, you might be doing these plays.'

But the lads who weren't getting picked, like me, Steve McManaman, Les Ferdinand, Rob Lee and Rio Ferdinand, were always messing about because we were disheartened. We even gave ourselves two nicknames: 'The Nuggets' for when we were sitting around, and 'The Dunga XI' for when we were playing practice games, because Dunga was the Brazilian captain at that time.

One morning, to lighten the mood, we'd written the names of players who were doing really well in the tournament on the back of our shirts. My squad number was 15, but I had 'Valderrama' scribbled across the shoulders in marker pen. On the pitch, Glenn was talking to the first team about what he wanted from corner kicks, but none of The Nuggets were listening. We were too busy laughing at our training tops. Valderrama, Ronaldo and Hagi were all sitting on the bench for England.

'Right, Number One is the near-post flick-on,' Glenn shouted. 'Number Two: aim the ball at someone round the back. Becks, do Number One ...'

While this was going on, The Nuggets were still fucking around, chatting, doing anything but watching the drills. Suddenly, Glenn heard the laughter and stopped play.

'What are you lot doing?' he shouted.

We all looked at each other like naughty schoolboys.

'Right, you lot, off,' he shouted, waving away the players on the pitch. 'You lot, on. Right, we're going to do Number One. Rio, what's Number One?'

Rio looked sheepish. 'Er, it's the one round the back?'

'No, it's not.'

Another Nugget suggested it was 'the one to the penalty spot'.

Glenn rolled his eyes. I knew he had the hump, but it was difficult for us to concentrate when we weren't getting time on the pitch. It was hard for me to stay focused when I was bored out of my mind.

France 1998 was the first tournament I'd been involved in where boozing wasn't a priority for me. Me and Tone shared a room, and it couldn't have been more different from the last time we bunked in together under Graham Taylor. In France we had a villa between us, with a kitchen and two bedrooms, but this time the doors stayed on their hinges. Tone was a lot calmer now that his drinking had stopped. He was learning French and taking piano lessons instead. The bloke who had been a million times over the limit when he'd crashed his car in 1990 had changed, big-time. He'd gone all intellectual and was talking quietly in *Countdown* Conundrum words. I couldn't understand him any more.

When it came to the food and nutrition, playing for Glenn was like being back with Arsenal. The players were taking all sorts of drinks and drugs, and none of them were giving me a buzz. The beer was replaced with vitamins and Chinese herbal remedies which were poured out of little glass tubes. There were lots of strange potions being given out, but I didn't have a clue what any of them did. It was all Wenger stuff, and we had to take our medicines at the right times, otherwise they wouldn't have the desired effect, whatever that was. It was very, very thorough. Nothing was left to chance.

The only problems were emotional ones. I'd see Lorraine from time to time and the kids would call up every now and then, but I soon realised that being away from my family for over a month was tough work. I'm sure that's what caused a lot of problems for Capello and the England squad when they went to South Africa in 2010. The boredom must have driven them all mad, but it's easily avoided. If Capello had talked to people like Glenn Hoddle and Terry Venables, and players like Tone and Alan Shearer who had captained the team in the past, it could have been sorted before they even left the country. He could have gone round to all of them and asked, 'Right, if you went to the World Cup again, what would you change? What worked and what didn't when you were there?' Capello would have learnt a lot about the pitfalls of managing a team in a long tournament abroad. Not to have taken in all the experience and opinions of people who had done it before was very naive.

When the squad first got together in La Manga, I noticed that a lot of the players stuck to their club cliques when they were relaxing at the hotel. The Man United boys – David Beckham, Gary Neville, Paul Scholes – would always sit together at dinner, likewise the Liverpool lot, but that seemed natural to me because I always hung around with people I knew rather than going out on a limb to mingle. If there were four or five mates from the club in the England squad it always made it easy for me.

By the time we'd got to France, everyone felt more comfortable and the players mixed up a bit more. I hung about with Rio, Michael Owen and the Arsenal crowd.

How Not To Be a Professional Footballer

Becks was a bloke that impressed me a lot, too. Despite the hype about him at the time, there was no Jack the lad in his character. Some people thought he was an arrogant kid, but they were wrong. He was just quiet, maybe even a bit shy.

He was brilliant footballer, too, he really was, but the reason he was such a great player for United, Real, AC Milan and England was that he practised. Whenever we were getting on to the coach from the training ground, I'd always look out of the window and he'd still be out there on his own in front of goal, practising free-kicks. He would spend an extra hour whipping balls over a dummy wall while the rest of us went back to the hotel. As I watched, he'd hit the target time after time after time. People didn't see that side of him, they thought his skill came naturally, but Becks practised more than anyone I'd ever met.

I spent a lot of time hanging around with Michael Owen, too. He was a top bloke, but annoyingly brilliant at every sport he played. Football, golf and snooker, Michael was like the eighties' cartoon character Sport Billy – he was blinding at everything. I sometimes wondered if he was a secret alcoholic because he was so sharp at pool. I was a good player, because I'd spent most of my life in pubs, but he used to slaughter me. After he'd spanked me 10–4 in a game, I'd think, 'I wonder if he has a drink problem?' You didn't get that good at pool unless you lived in a boozer. It later turned out he had a table in his house.

Do Not Ask Eileen Drewery for a Short Back and Sides

I remember Sport Billy was a bit fed up one day because some weirdo had sent him a letter. A bloke had made out that he'd been sleeping with his missus while he was away. I had to give him a bit of advice and warn him about the nutters. I told him something that had happened to me few months earlier when a drunk bloke had approached me and made out that I'd owed him some money. He reckoned he was going to shoot me over it. I knew he was making it up, but it showed me some of the crap I'd have to put up with because of my reputation. That seemed to cheer Michael up. When a player gets drama for the first time, they think they're the only person in the world to have gone through it. It was good for him to hear that other footballers got it too. Then he stuffed me at pool again.

It's hard work being stuck in the middle of nowhere and feeling bored shitless. It was that dull being away with England that Sport Billy and me must have played well over a thousand games of pool. There was nothing else to do. I was never one for computer games, and Tone kept beating me on pinball in the hotel arcade, so I had a choice of either getting spanked at pool or waxing the dolphin. The daily routine of eating, training, relaxing and eating again actually made me a little bit depressed.

It helped that the World Cup matches were on the telly, because it meant we could have a bet, but nobody went too crazy with their money, not even me. And even if I had lost it and put some silly money down, I was never going to win big. Al Shearer and Teddy were the book-makers that year, and they were as tight as you like. The only time they got taken to the cleaners was when Holland beat South Korea 5-0. The pair of them had writ-ten Cocu in at 14/1 to score the first goal, and quite a few had taken it up. When Holland popped the first one away and everyone realised Cocu had got it, Al and Teddy looked pretty gutted.

On the pitch we started off well in France. Tunisia were beaten 2-0, and Scholesy got a great goal even though it was boiling hot that day, a thousand degrees, but in the next game Romania beat us 2-1. It was a massive shock. Nobody knew what had happened for us to lose to them. It meant that we had to beat Colombia to go through to the knockout stages, but I knew we'd do them. The odds on us winning were 4/5 and I should have put a massive bet on, but for some reason I didn't. It was probably Eileen's talk of demons and bad spirits that had put me off. I was right about Becks, though: his practice sessions made perfect and he scored a great free-kick as we won 2-0 to set up a second-round tie against Argentina.

What a match that was. England versus Argentina in 1998 was one of the greatest games I'd seen in World Cup football and it was a buzz to be part of it. Sport Billy also scored one of the best international goals ever when he ran around a million Argentinian defenders in the first half and banged the ball away. His run started on the half-way line. I was off my seat, applauding – I couldn't believe what I'd seen. We knew he could do stuff like that, because he'd skinned most of us in training, and he'd been fearless during his first season with Liverpool, but to do it in a World Cup game against some of the best defenders on the planet? That took some neck. He was so fast that the Argentinians couldn't even hack him down in time. Every defender in the game was terrified of him after that because he was double quick.

It was 2–2 at half-time, but the game really turned on its head in the second half when Becks kicked out at Diego Simeone, the Argentinian midfielder. Simeone had fouled him, pushing Becks in the back and bringing him down, but while on the floor, Becks lashed out with his boot. It was only a flick of the foot, and it was stupid, but the ref sent him off, waving his red card and pointing to the tunnel. Like Becks didn't know where it was – he'd walked down it to get to the pitch in the first place.

On the touchline we were furious. The lad hardly touched Simeone, who was an idiot and was looking to cause trouble. When Becks got home a few weeks later, the press had ripped him to shreds, and the fans were chucking abuse. There were effigies of him hanging from lampposts and people were booing him wherever he went. I couldn't believe it, he'd only lost his head for a second, and it wasn't as if he'd punched anyone or cut Simeone in half during a tackle. Still, it didn't really affect his career or his game the way it would have with some players. Becks went on to be one of the world's best. It takes a lot of character to come through all that flak and become a world-class footballer – I couldn't talk highly enough of the bloke.

It gave me a break too, and after Becks's sending-off, Glenn put me on in the second half with 15 minutes to go. It was the first time I'd been involved in the tournament. The game was still poised at 2–2 and we soon crept into extra time. In the dying minutes, Sol Campbell scored a cracking header from a corner, but it was disallowed because Al Shearer had apparently fouled a defender.

It was to get much worse, though. When extra time was finished, Glenn walked on to the pitch and announced his penalty takers: Al, Incey, Michael, David Batty and ... me.

Me.

Me with the demons and the fear of flying and the panic attacks. Me with the nervous wee. There I was, standing on the halfway line, getting ready to take a penalty against Argentina, bricking it. Can you imagine that? It was probably the biggest game I'd ever played in, but all I could think about was a penalty I'd taken three months earlier at Bramall Lane. Boro versus Sheffield United in the League. It was a Tuesday night game, we were 1-0 down and the ref gave us a penalty. I was Robbo's spot-kick taker, but as I stepped up to take it, my head went. It was the first time the fear of missing had ever affected me as a player. The goal shrank and I knew I wouldn't score. It was the weirdest thing that had ever happened to me in my career.

As the confidence drained out of me at Sheffield United, I knew I was done for, but I couldn't exactly turn round to the other lads with an excuse: 'Not tonight, gents. Someone else take it.' They would have thought I'd gone mad, but I should have followed my gut instinct. Normally when I miss a pen it's because the keeper's saved it – seriously, there's no excuse for missing the target from such a short distance – but this time I booted it 40 yards over the bar. It was a howler.

These days, watching on the telly on *Soccer Saturday*, I can see if a player's going to score when he steps up to take a penalty. It's written all over his face. Nine times out of ten I'm bang on. It comes from experience: before my pen against Argentina, the fear was written all over me because I couldn't get Bramall Lane out of my head. I watched Al step up to score his spot-kick. Then Incey missed his. I got nervy.

'I'm going to let down my wife, my kids, Mum and Dad, my team-mates, my whole country,' I thought.

It was awful. Glenn could see it, like he'd sussed out my fear of flying on that plane to Casablanca. He walked up to me, placed his hand on my chest and stared me in the eyes.

'You.'

'Will.'

'Not.'

'Miss,' he said slowly.

I thought, 'Thank fuck for that. Glenn's said I'm going to score, I'll be fine. And if I do miss, now I'm blaming Glenn, because he's told me I'm going to be OK.'

I was up next. I walked down towards the area, in front of all the fans, and placed the ball on the spot. When I looked up, the goal was as big as you like, it was huge, I couldn't believe it. Glenn had worked his magic and I knew I couldn't miss. Even when their keeper, Carlos Roa, started playing funny games with the ref, arguing about this and that, I didn't care.

'Don't go playing your joker on me, pal,' I thought. 'You haven't got a chance. Glenn's told me I'm going to score.'

I stepped back and fired the ball home, and even though the keeper went the right way, the ball was in the top corner. He didn't stand a chance. The truth was, Glenn had helped me to put it there, I'd been touched by The Hand of Hodd. It was like seeing Nick Faldo on that flight. I knew then that my plane wasn't going to fall out of the sky. When Glenn touched me on the chest, my chances of scoring were slashed from 1,000,000/1 to odds-on.

Do Not Ask Eileen Drewery for a Short Back and Sides

Moments later, David Batty missed his kick and we were out of the tournament. Maybe if he'd been as scatty as me and chatted to Glenn before his spot-kick, we might have gone further. After the game the mood in the dressing-room was down, nobody spoke, but if there was anyone you wanted to miss a penalty it was David Batty, because he had his life in perspective. It wasn't going to ruin his world or bring him down for ever. His attitude was, 'I took a penalty, I stepped up, and I missed. Next.' He was a brilliant footballer and it wasn't going to consume him, he could cope with the disappointment. There are a lot of players who wouldn't have done. Me, most probably. I'd have cracked up for a while.

Glenn knew we'd been unlucky. We'd lost on pens, which was always a lottery. Sol Campbell had scored a goal and it was disallowed for a nothing foul by Shearer. Becks had been sent off. People said afterwards that if we'd beaten Argentina we'd have won the World Cup. Well, maybe, but we still would have needed to beat Holland after that, and then Brazil or France, so it was a tough call. It wasn't like we were playing Macedonia and Moldova on our way to the final.

It didn't help, though. We were on our way back to England. On the flight home, I got chatting to Becks.

'What are you going to do now, mate?' I asked. 'Holiday or something?'

How Not To Be a Professional Footballer

He went, 'Oh yeah, I'm off to see Posh Spice in New York.'

Fucking hell, I thought. All right for some. I'm going back to my *Truman Show* life in the Northeast.

Do Not Give Gazza the Keys to the Team Bus

'Merse moves to Aston Villa and becomes a second son to Deadly Doug.'

When I got back to Boro nothing had changed. Lorraine still wouldn't move up to the Northeast and I was away from the family, with only Gaz and my brother as house-mates. After a difficult start, I'd had a good first season at The Riverside, playing-wise, but when the World Cup finished I could feel the walls closing in on me again. Middlesbrough is a lonely place when you're a million miles away from your wife and kids. Anywhere in England is. I was still really homesick and beginning to feel scared. Another blow-out on the booze seemed just around the corner.

I went back to see Eileen Drewery. She started to get my head straight, but as the season got underway, I could feel the pressure building. In pre-season, my panic attacks started to come back; as I went to sleep at night, voices in my head kept telling me I was a shit player, that I was done for.

'Give it up, Merse.'

'Oi, Merse, you can't do it any more, not up here in Boro.'

Eileen calmed me down in her meetings, but every day I wanted to get paro and blow a few quid in the bookies. It wasn't long before I crumbled.

Step one was to chuck £10,000 on some Scottish football games, a rugby league match and the horses.

Step two was to get bang on the beers again.

One afternoon in pre-season, I met up with Gazza and Chris Waddle on a golf course near Newcastle for a game, but the last thing on my mind was putting and fairway irons. By the ninth hole I was knocking back all sorts of shots. As the evening came to a messy end in a Newcastle bar, I was sinking vodka and Red Bulls. I was well and truly off the wagon, as one or two more heavy nights followed, but I pulled myself together and started going to AA meetings. I also began reading books by former drinkers like Ian 'Lovejoy' McShane and Eric Clapton. Their stories helped me through, but I was so unsettled that I felt like a bloke standing on the edge of a cliff. I was looking down, and a million miles below were the rocks. One gust of wind could have blown me over.

Do Not Give Gazza the Keys to the Team Bus

Then it really kicked off. A tabloid newspaper ran a story claiming I wanted to leave Boro because of the drinking and gambling culture at the club, but how could I complain of a drinking and gambling culture? I used to drink like a fish. When I'd gambled big in the past, I was putting over £15,000 or £20,000. That lot were betting 30 quid a go, a oner on pay day. I could hardly talk.

I knew where the story had come from. It was that old chestnut 'the source' shooting his mouth off in the papers, and I guessed who it was. A former mate of mine had stitched me up, but it was all bollocks. Straight away, though, Gaz had the hump because he thought I was having a pop at him. Robbo also wanted to know what was going on. When I explained to him that I'd been dropped in it, he understood, but the atmosphere wasn't great at first.

'There's some drinking and some serious gambling going on, but it isn't anything that you should be bothered about, Boss,' I said. 'But it's everything for me to worry over.'

Then a couple of weeks into the season I got a call telling me that Aston Villa were interested in signing me. Well, I was up for that, because they were a big club and a hell of a lot nearer to St Albans than Boro. They were also an established Premiership team. Andy Townsend, who was big mates with John Gregory, the Aston Villa manager, had already told me, 'Villa would be interested in you,' and I knew then that it was just the move I needed.

I eventually signed for £6.75 million, and there were no hard feelings between me and the gaffer. Robbo has been great about it ever since, we've stayed friends and we always talk whenever we see each other. It's like nothing ever happened. He knew I'd done a job for him and helped the club to get promotion. I honestly think people underestimated Bryan Robson at that time. Everyone who went up to Boro played because of that bloke, no question. I know I did. I'm not being horrible, but no one went up there and signed because it was Middlesbrough Football Club, they went up there to play for Robbo. He was also helped by the chairman, Steve Gibson. He made sure the manager got pretty much everything he needed to run the team and did a phenomenal job of putting Boro on the map. I'm a great believer that we shouldn't give things away in sport. Honestly, they knight cricketers for winning a game these days, but Steve Gibson should be Sir Steve in my opinion.

I find it extraordinary that the crowds disappeared when Boro went down recently, because I remember when I played up there against QPR on a Friday night, the Riverside was packed to the rafters with 38,000 people. West London is 250 miles away, it was a Division One game. In 2010, during a game with Leeds there was no one there, it was dead. Leeds filled the whole away end and the rest of the ground was a graveyard. I thought it was tragic.

The fans were less forgiving towards me than Robbo had been. As soon as I left, they were moaning. I was hated, they were making out that I'd let them down. I thought, 'Fucking hell, how does that work?' I'd gone to Boro and done a job for them. The team was promoted, but I was the bad boy when I left. Juninho did it the other way round. He went there, they got relegated and then he left them behind, but he was a bloody hero afterwards. And don't forget I'd left a big, big club to play for a Division One team. I'd learnt for the first time in my career that there was no pleasing some people.

Typically, there was plenty of disaster to deal with before I moved to Birmingham, and a lot of it revolved around Gazza. A couple of weeks before my transfer, Boro played Villa away (of all teams) and as the lads got together at the training ground, Gaz offered to head down to the betting shop to put on some bets for everyone. It was something he occasionally did. The lads found that having a small flutter helped to quicken up the journey.

The club had brought a brand new coach, and it must have cost about a gazillion quid because it had on it just about every appliance known to man – TVs, fridges, the lot. We were all looking forward to making our first journey, but as it sat gleaming in the club car park, Gazza noticed that the keys had been left in the ignition. He hopped in. Then he started up the engine and began the one-mile drive to the nearest high street while the rest of us pissed ourselves laughing. He didn't get very far. When he got to the end of the road that led out of the training ground, he turned right and crashed the bus into a concrete bollard.

The side of the coach was caved in and the locks on the compartments that contained our kit for the match had been mangled, so the doors were wedged shut.

'Bloody hell, Gaz, what have you done?' I shouted as we all walked round the side of the coach to look at the damage.

We ended up on another coach and having some new shirts sent straight to Birmingham for the match. Meanwhile, when the news reached our coach driver, he started shitting himself. A big fuss had been made of our new bus when the club bought it, but Gaz had wrecked it before the team had made a journey on the motorway. The funny thing was, Robbo didn't seem to care. Gazza was allowed to pay for the damage out of his next pay packet and nothing more was said.

Even as I settled in at Villa there was drama. I got a call telling me Gazza had been taken into care at The Priory in London. His boozing was out of control, and some of the doctors there thought it would be a good idea if I went in to talk to him. I knew from my own experience that it was a shock for people when they first went into rehab. Gazza wouldn't have known what was happening; he would have been all over the shop mentally. They figured a friendly face might do him good.

Then the weirdest thing happened. As we were sitting in his room chatting, guitar legend Eric Clapton walked in. Oh my God, I couldn't believe it, I thought I was hallucinating. I stared at him, thinking he'd come into the wrong room by accident, but it was no mistake. It turned out that 'Slowhand' was also a volunteer helper at the hospital. I'd just finished reading his bloody book, so I was well freaked out, though I was a bit gutted that we hadn't got another pop star, like All Saints or Geri Halliwell.

'All right, Eric, what are you doing here?' I stammered as he walked in.

Apparently when the story had broken in the papers that Gazza had been admitted, Eric had called up the hospital. He asked if he could talk to him because he figured he could give him some advice. Years later, in 2008, he would even offer Gaz the chance of checking into his Crossroads rehab centre, which is based in Antigua. He obviously wanted to help him out. After half an hour of bedside chat, Eric got up to buy coffees for everyone. Then Gazza rolled over in his bed and gave me a funny look.

'Who the fuck is that?' he said.

I couldn't believe it. One of the most famous men in rock history was bringing him a coffee, and Gaz didn't have a bloody clue.

I played at Aston Villa for four years and most of the time I loved it there, but typically it took a while for me to settle in. I thought I'd be able to commute to Birmingham from St Albans and still live with Lorraine and the kids, but as with Boro it wasn't working out for me. The gaffer, John Gregory, was nowhere near as understanding as Robbo had been at first and we didn't see eye to eye at all. He thought I was being all drama about not moving up, and he started making life difficult for me.

'We're all in tomorrow for training,' he'd say to the lads on a Tuesday afternoon. I'd spend a couple of hours driving in the next day, dodging the traffic, my back playing up, but when I got to the training ground, all we'd do was have a bath or a massage. I moaned my head off.

'What the fuck are you bringing me up here for?'

'Well, you should be living up here,' he said. 'It wouldn't have been a problem then.'

He was right, but it all seemed a bit petty. When we were beaten 2–0 by Fulham in the FA Cup fourth round, he called us all in for an extra training session the next day because he wasn't happy with our performance.

Do Not Give Gazza the Keys to the Team Bus

'Fuck off,' I grumbled under my breath. 'Sunday? What difference is that going to make? We've been beaten, we can't change it.'

Jim Walker was the club's physio at the time. He would later become my assistant manager at Walsall. He'd over-heard me bellyaching.

'Oh, you big-time Charlie,' he said. 'You're in, what's the difference? In my day, [former Spurs and Derby legend] Dave Mackay would never have complained about train-ing on a Sunday.'

I was so angry, I hadn't heard him properly.

'Oh fuck off, Jim, what's he got to do with it? He sang "American Pie".'

Some of the lads started sniggering. Our goalkeeper, Mark Bosnich, leant over to me as I was changing.

'Merse, Jim said Dave Mackay, not Don McLean.'

The funny thing was, despite the rucking, Villa were flying. We didn't lose until 21 November (to Liverpool) and we were top of the table until Boxing Day. After we'd beaten Southampton 4–1 away, a week before the Liver-pool game, we'd taken the club's record unbeaten streak in the League to 12 games. As we were walking off at the final whistle, John started ordering us back on to the field. I thought he wanted us to thank the fans, but for some reason the club had organised a photo shoot to celebrate the new record. I was pissed off. You won't see me anywhere in that photo because I was at the back, hiding.

How Not To Be a Professional Footballer

'I'm not having any of this,' I thought.

Sure, we were top of the League and winning games, but everybody at the club was getting carried away. A month or so after the Southampton result, we were four games without a win and had to face Arsenal. I couldn't play because I was suffering from a bad back (that commute in the car again), but I watched us claw back a two-goal deficit to win 3–2. It was a great victory, but in training the following week you'd have thought we'd won the League, judging by how some of the lads were behaving.

'Everyone should calm down a bit here,' I said in the dressing-room. 'We'll be lucky if we finish 10 points behind Arsenal.'

Everyone turned on me. 'Shut up, Merse! You don't know what you're talking about.'

The lads were really giving it, but I was worried that a lot of them didn't understand the winning mentality needed to finish top in the Premiership. I was right too. At the end of the season, Arsenal were second, and we finished sixth, missing out on a UEFA Cup spot. Arsenal were 23 points ahead of us.

Away from the pitch it was business as usual: I was gambling. Me and the missus separated, eventually getting divorced. I would later marry my second wife Louise and we had twins, two daughters. All of that in the space of four years. I was up and down all the time and, as you've probably learnt by now, when I'm down I gamble big-time.

Because of my bad back, I was starting to miss games, and when it made me unavailable one Saturday, shortly after the 3–2 win over Arsenal, I asked our physio if I could have a break away rather than travelling with the team to watch the game.

'Jim, I'm not sitting on a coach for three hours with my back,' I said. 'There's no point. I might try to get away for the weekend instead. What do you think?'

'Yeah, good idea,' he said, though I reckon he thought I'd be spending the time with the kids at home. Instead I booked a flight to New York on Concorde. The ticket cost me seven grand, the hotel in Manhattan a couple of grand more. As soon as I landed, I backed the New York Jets to win in the play-offs against Jacksonville at 10/11. I bet £11,000. I knew that if the Jets came in, my winnings would pay for the whole trip and then some. If they lost, it was a bloody expensive holiday.

Luckily for me, they came in. But when I went back to Villa for training a few days later, I was called into the gaffer's office. It turned out that someone had spotted me at the airport. They had grassed me up. I was fined two weeks' wages, which was about £50,000 at the time. Instead of getting a free holiday and a few quid in my pocket, I was well down.

How Not To Be a Professional Footballer

It wasn't just the club that were having a moan, it was the papers as well. A few writers in the national newspapers were having a pop at me over the New York incident. When one of them turned up at the training ground, probably to interview one of the other players, somebody clocked him in the canteen.

'Oi, Merse,' he said. 'That's the bloke who slaughtered you the other week.'

I was furious. I had to save face, so I steamed over to him in my shorts and flip-flops and pinned him up against the wall. I was that angry.

I said, 'Don't start printing stuff about me like that.'

'It's not me!' he yelped as I held him in a Darth Vader grip. 'It's not bloody me.'

'Bollocks it's not ...'

But he was right, I'd got the wrong bloke. I felt like a right wally, and I was tripping over myself for weeks to be nice to the geezer whenever he turned up at press conferences. I don't know what was wrong with me at the time. Thank God I never bumped into Dave Mackay. I would have probably got him to sign my copy of 'American Pie'.

When I first showed up at Villa I thought we had a weird old dressing-room. I was a recovering alcoholic, drug addict and compulsive gambler. Then there was our striker, Stan Collymore. Stan was a depressive; a great player who could be one of the best footballers in the country when he was in the mood, but a high-maintenance character. One minute he was the happiest person in the world and would chat the hind legs off a donkey. The next he wouldn't talk to you for days. I'd say, 'Morning Stan,' and he'd walk past me like he'd never seen me before in his life.

Still, Stan was nothing compared with our keeper, Mark Bosnich, who was a right headbanger. He later admitted to having a serious cocaine habit, and was once fined £1,000 by the FA for making a Nazi salute towards a section of Spurs fans. I remember that we used to wear special heart-rate monitors at Villa. They were connected to a wristwatch so we could see how our tickers were reacting to the training. Sometimes we would have to stop working if our heart rates were too quick. Apparently we would be doing ourselves more harm than good if we carried on running around. We used to wear them at home too. One morning I went into training and Bozzy wasn't there. By 11 o'clock he still hadn't arrived. One of the coaches rang his house, and Bozzy answered, saying, 'I got up and when I looked at the heart-rate monitor it was too high, so I went back to bed again.'

That's what he was like. I remember our midfielder, Alan Thompson, once squirted him with his water bottle as we were getting ready for training. 'I'm not having that,' shouted Bozzy, and he got dressed and went home.

How Not To Be a Professional Footballer

It wasn't a total nuthouse; we had some more level-headed players as well. Gareth Southgate was a very good defender, a lot better than people gave him credit for. I could tell he was going to be a manager, even then, because he loved his football. He understood the game and he was a good leader on and off the pitch. He was intelligent. Ugo Ehiogu was a great player in defence, and later we had David James in goal, who turned out to be a top-drawer keeper, though he was capable of the odd blunder.

The chairman was great too. He loved me like a son. Not long after I'd signed, he also bought striker Dion Dublin for £5.75 million, and in his first few games he scored seven goals, including a hat-trick against Southampton. He looked like a great signing. In 2001, somebody mentioned to me how much he was getting and it was a lot. I thought, 'Hang on, that's more than me.'

At the time, I was captain of the team, so I called up the club chairman, 'Deadly' Doug Ellis, the night before we were due to fly to Europe to play in the Intertoto Cup.

'I said, I ain't going. I'm not having that. How's Dion getting more than me?'

Doug was confused. 'What do you mean?'

'I'm not having it. I'm not having Dion getting more money than me.'

It had nothing to do with Dion, but I thought I was entitled to more money because the gaffer had made me captain.

Do Not Give Gazza the Keys to the Team Bus

'You've got to go,' pleaded Doug.

'I'm not going. I haven't got to go.'

He said, 'Please go over, get on the plane and I will fly over with the chief executives and we'll come to your hotel room and sort everything out.'

'Make sure you do,' I said. 'Don't make me go over there and then not turn up.'

But, to be fair, they showed up and sorted it out. Doug got a lot of stick at Villa, but I just don't see what the problem was. Some fans seem to think that he held the club back, but he spent loads of money. Villa's problem was that they spent it on some pretty average players. For example, Alan Thompson cost them £4.5 million from Bolton and he was way out of his league. He even used to say it in training. He'd be in the canteen going, 'I'm out of my depth here.' Defender Steve Watson was another. These were good professionals, but they weren't going to push Villa up to the next level.

We came close to success at Villa, but there were never any cigars flying around. We never really got near to winning the League, there were always a handful of teams that were just that much better than us, but we were a strong top six side. After a frosty first season, me and John Gregory started to get on a lot better, though that was mainly due to the fact that I eventually bit the bullet and moved into an apartment in Birmingham. My form improved straight away, just like it had done at Boro.

How Not To Be a Professional Footballer

That year, 1999–2000, was the closest I got to winning silverware with Villa. After another OK season in the League, where we finished sixth again, we also steered the team to an FA Cup Final against Chelsea. It would be the last FA Cup Final to be held at the old Wembley. We worked our way there by beating Darlington (2–1), South-ampton (1–0), Leeds (3–2) , Everton (2–1) and Bolton on penalties in the semi-final. But in the final we were too negative, it was crap. We went out to defend and Chelsea nicked the game 1–0. The only thing I could say about that final was that it was a shit old game.

I seriously considered retiring from football around that time. I'd been suffering from injuries, and things were getting to me off the pitch, what with the divorce from Lorraine going on in the background. I was fed up with playing. I mentioned it to the press one day, and there was a bit of a fuss. Thankfully, *Match of the Day* gave me a boost a week or two later. On the show, pundit Mark Lawrenson presented some clips of me playing for Villa and highlighted some of my midfield play during a Premier League game.

'If he's thinking of retiring then he should watch this and reconsider,' he said.

Lawro was right. I was still up for it; the only problem was that Villa weren't. We were an all right side, but we could never live up to the expectations of the fans. In the 2000–01 season we ended up drawing 15 matches, which was incredible really, and we ended up in eighth place, which wasn't good enough.

In the end, the pressure got to John Gregory. The following season we blew a two-goal lead in the FA Cup third round against Man United at home and his face was a picture on the touchline. He looked gutted. Then the 'Gregory Out' banners started appearing at the ground. Any manager will tell you, when fans have spent a morning painting slogans on an old picnic blanket, that's when the writing's on the wall. The tin tack's just around the corner.

I'd grown to like John, and I think he thought I was all right too. In the end we got on. Once I'd moved to Birmingham, he could see I wanted to put a shift in for the club, and I was scoring some cracking goals for the team. He often called me into his office to talk about the game ahead, or this, that and the other. He knew I liked to be involved. But being pally with the players wasn't enough to turn the ship around, and in January 2002, he walked. He reckoned the pressure had got to him and he couldn't take it any more.

I couldn't blame him. I'd been there as well, but as a player. I knew how hard it was to concentrate when everything was coming down on you as a person. It was a bloody nightmare. John decided he quite fancied a quieter life, which was fair enough. The only problem was that his departure would have a big impact on my Villa career.

Do Not Tell Harry Redknapp You're Going into Rehab only to Bunk off to Barbados for a Jolly

'Merse joins up with Portsmouth. Cue two funny phone calls and a bungled holiday on the beach.'

I was devastated when John Gregory walked out on Aston Villa, absolutely gutted. Even though we hadn't really seen eye to eye when I first signed for the club, I'd grown to like him. In the end I thought he was a top, top manager. But Doug Ellis wasn't planning on wasting any time before getting a new arse into the Villa hot seat, and the minute John had driven away from the club car park, I was called into the chairman's office.

'Who do you think should be the manager, Merse?' he said. 'Is there anyone around that you think could do a job for us?'

I wasn't sure, but my old England gaffer, Graham Taylor, was back at Villa Park. He was working as a non-executive director, and although we hadn't exactly got on at international level, I thought he could do a good job in filling John's shoes.

'What about Graham Taylor, Mr Chairman?' I said. 'He knows the club inside out because he's managed here before. He also knows the kids like Lee Hendrie, Gareth Barry and Darius Vassell because he's been working here. He'd be spot on.'

Doug nodded and Graham Taylor was put in charge straight away. I thought that was fast moving, but I fell out with the new gaffer even faster once we started working together again. It was my fault really, I should have kept my mouth shut, but in his first meeting with the lads, Graham started banging on about what he'd done at Watford and how he was going to do it again at Villa.

It was an impressive story. At the age of 32, which was pretty young for a manager, Graham took over at Vicarage Road and led the team from the old Fourth Division to the old First Division in five years. Most teams would have been spanked having gone up to the top flight, but Watford finished second in their first ever season as a

Division One club in 1983. They even qualified for the UEFA Cup. A year later, Graham got them to the FA Cup Final, which they lost 2–0 to Everton. It was top, top work, and all of it was down to him. The only problem was that we weren't Watford and it wasn't 1983 any more.

Silly bollocks here started laughing with a couple of the lads, making comments, joking around. I remembered the hours of throw-ins we'd been forced to watch on video replay when I was an England player and was praying to God that I wouldn't have to go through that 'mare again. As the giggling got louder, Graham wanted to know what was so funny.

'Come on, Gaffer,' I said. 'It's 2002, this isn't going to wash.'

Graham glared at me. I could tell he had the right hump about it. A lot of the younger players looked up to me at that time, and many of them came to me for advice on this, that and the other. I was also team captain, so a lot of the senior lads listened to what I had to say as well. Probably the gaffer thought I was acting up and being a bad influence, and I reckon he must have marked my card. While I stayed the skipper of the team as Villa cruised to an average eighth spot in the League in 2002, by pre-season that summer I was sitting on the bench. I was well unhappy about it.

Doug Ellis wasn't too bothered about my demotion; he figured I'd be back in the side soon enough. He even called one night as I sat indoors sulking. He wanted to reassure me.

'Don't worry, Merse, you'll be playing again soon, you've got to be,' he said.

He bloody loved me, the chairman, but clearly Graham didn't share his affection because for a whole summer I sat on the bench, fuming, trying to work out what I had to do to get a game. I was called into the manager's office before the first day of the 2002–03 campaign.

'Merse, what are you doing?' he said. 'You're not in the team ...'

I told him I wasn't bothered because Doug had said that I'd be playing sooner rather than later. Graham went ballistic over that. He hated the thought of the chairman talking to me and making plans behind his back.

'You're not in my plans,' he shouted. 'How much money do you want the club to pay you to go?'

I thought he was pulling my leg.

'Nothing, I don't want to go,' I said. 'I love it here, boss.'

It was true; I did love it at Villa. When I was at Arsenal as a youngster, I hadn't appreciated what a wonderful club it had been until I'd left and signed for Boro. Villa was the closest thing to Arsenal I'd known since, but this time I was old enough to appreciate the people, the fans and the history of the team. I really wanted to stay, but I could see that Graham had other ideas.

'Well, you're not playing now,' he said. 'It doesn't look like you're going to be playing in the future either, so you might as well consider my offer.'

I said, 'If you're going to be like that, what about £100,000 then?'

Graham got out of his seat. 'Sounds fine. Give me 10 minutes.'

He walked out of the office and called Doug. I couldn't believe it – he was actually going to get the dough for me. One hundred grand was a yankee for me in those days, but my world was spinning, I was leaving a team that I loved.

'Fuck,' I thought. 'Why didn't I ask for £200,000?'

I knew right then I could have got more money out of him, because Graham couldn't have jumped out of his seat any faster. Moments later he walked back into the room with a cheque for £100,000 in his hands and I was out of the club. I was devastated, I thought my world was about to fall apart, and I didn't have a clue where I was going to go next. As I drove home I could see the scrapheap looming and I didn't want to be on it. I knew I had at least another year in the Premiership and I was leaving Villa too early. I sat on my sofa that afternoon and cried my eyes out. Then the phone started to ring. It was Harry Redknapp.

Do Not Tell Harry Redknapp . . .

HARRY: Hello, Merse, Harry Redknapp here.

ME: Hello, Harry. What are you up to?

HARRY: I'm in charge at Pompey now, son. What about you?

ME: Well, I'm sitting around, scratching my cods, because Villa have let me go. What are Pompey like?

HARRY: (And, God's honest truth, these were Harry's exact words.) They're fucking shit, son. They finish in the bottom half every year, they always have to win one of their last games to stay up. I've come in and I can't believe how shit they are. I've got rid of all the players, I've kept Nigel Quashie and I've brought in a whole new team on free transfers. Now I need a player like you, Merse. Come down, I'll make you captain and we'll have a right fucking go.

ME: I've got to stop you there, Harry. I'm married again now. I've got twins in Birmingham. I'm not moving the family down for a two-year contract, and I don't want to be travelling down to the coast every day to train, not at my age.

HARRY: Fine. I'll tell you what, son: don't work Mondays, don't work Wednesdays and don't work Fridays. Just make sure you turn it on for me when Saturday comes.

ME: I like the sound of that.

HARRY: You won't get the wages you were on at Villa.

ME: Well, that's William Hill's loss, not mine. Let them worry about that. Gaffer, I'll sign.

How Not To Be a Professional Footballer

It happened double quick. I was a Pompey player, joining a team of free transfers and midfielder Nigel Quashie. Thanks to Graham, I'd scored £100,000 in betting money that day, too. By the time I'd put the blower down, my tears had dried double quick.

Harry was clever with his free transfers because he hadn't just dragged in eight bargain-basement wingers and two defenders for nothing; he'd nabbed 10 specific players, one for each position in the team. Well, apart from the spot taken by Nigel Quashie. The way the gaffer had talked him up, I reckoned Nigel must have been a better player than Dennis Bergkamp and Gazza put together. Elsewhere, the teamsheet was pretty strong: former West Ham keeper Shaka Hislop was in goal, and as well as muggins here, Harry had brought in former internationals Steve Stone and Tim Sherwood (who signed in January 2003) to toughen the side up in the middle of the park. By Championship standards we had a pretty good team.

My only problem was that Pompey and Villa were dog and duck. It was like going back to Brentford. The players had to do everything themselves. I even had to wash my own training stuff every day, until Kev the kit man offered a deal to all the players. For £50 a week he'd do their laundry for them, and that included training gear and match shirts, the works.

Do Not Tell Harry Redknapp . . .

I thought £50 a week was a bit steep, so I figured on being a bit cheeky with Kev. I'd taken a massive pay cut from what I'd been receiving at Aston Villa, but there was a bonus clause that stated I'd receive £250,000 if we won promotion to the Premiership at the end of the season. I'm not being funny, a quarter mill was a nice amount of money to get as bonus, but it was also a big gamble considering Harry had told me the team usually finished in the bottom half every year. Pompey hadn't been in the top flight for about 500 years, and the gaffer could have offered me £10 million for all I cared. I never reckoned we would get to the Premiership, not when I first signed anyway.

I gave Kev an alternative offer. 'I'll tell you what I'll do, mate,' I said. 'If you wash my kit for the rest of the season for nothing, I'll give you ten grand if we go up.'

I thought I was on to a winner, and Kev nearly bit my hand off. As the campaign got underway and the team went on a winning streak, he'd come into training every day with a smile on his face. He could smell his money. The fans were buzzing as well. Suddenly Pompey were on the up. In my first game we smashed Nottingham Forest 2-0, and though there was only 19,000 people in the ground it sounded like 100,000 had crammed into the seats. Fratton Park was like the Nou Camp or Old Trafford, it was that loud.

I hadn't played in front of anything like it in my life. The fans never stopped singing, some bloke was ringing a bell all game – it was phenomenal. I knew right then I'd come to a special place. The team might have finished in the bottom half last season, but they still had enough paying punters to fill the entire stadium.

The following week I hit the ground with a bump. We played Palace away and for the first 45 minutes we took one hell of a battering. When the half-time whistle went we were 2–0 down and I couldn't see any other result than an embarrassing defeat, because by rights it should have been 100–0. I thought they were going to put four or five past us in the second half, no problems. As I walked off the pitch, I started to sulk.

'What the fuck have I done coming here?' I moaned. 'Don't tell me it's one of them ones where we win one week and get battered the next ...'

On the way to the dressing-room, I thought Harry was going to go mental in his half-time talk, but he was much more savvy than that. He started pointing his fingers at players and dishing out orders.

'You off, you off and you off,' he shouted.

'We're going three at the back, two wing-backs.'

He pointed at me.

'Merse, you go in the hole, have a free role, we play two up front.'

When we ran out again, we were a completely different team. Harry had seen what was going wrong on the park and sorted it out as quickly as he could. There was no pussyfooting around. He was unreal. We scored three goals in the second half and won 3-2, the winning goal coming in the last minute. We were unrecognisable from the side that had rolled over in the first half.

The win was down to the manager, he was obviously a top-drawer reader of the game, like George had been at Arsenal. Some people might make out that Harry is a lucky gaffer, but that's bollocks. His football knowledge is so sharp it's scary, and the reason things sometimes go his way, like the last-minute winner against Palace, is that he's so clued up. He attacks teams on the pitch. In the transfer market he's not afraid to take a punt on a player who might appear over the hill to other managers. He knows that they could probably do a job for him. And if that player is free, like I was, then what's he got to lose?

It also makes me sick when people describe him as a wheeler-dealer, because when he does sign people, he buys them to play in a particular position. He doesn't do a Man City or a Chelsea. He won't grab every Tom, Dick and Harry just because they're available and then not play them even though they've been signed for £35 zillion quid each. He's shrewder than that. Honestly, the only way I can see England winning the World Cup in the next 10 years is if Harry's in charge. He's that good.

With the gaffer's football brain, the results kept on going our way. We went on a roll and Pompey started beating everybody in sight. I loved it, but I think Kev the kit man loved it more. We started marching up the table. In the new year we picked up some great results. We beat Grimsby 3-0 and Derby 6-2 in February, then we banged in five goals against Millwall at their place, not that anyone was there to see it. There had been some naughty history between the two sets of fans. Our lot had been banned from the New Den and the away end was empty, which was a shame because I had a blinder, even scoring a penalty. I played so well that when Harry subbed me five minutes before the end of the game the whole ground rose to their feet. I was given a standing ovation by the entire stadium, and there wasn't even a Pompey supporter in the place. After the final whistle, as I was signing autographs on my way back to the team coach, an old bloke wanted to shake my hand.

'I've been coming here 50 years, son,' he said. 'I've never seen a performance as good as yours.'

That meant a lot to me. People can think what they like about Millwall fans, but I've always known them as a crowd that appreciate good football. And they don't applaud too many opponents off that pitch, I can tell you.

One of our biggest days came in the FA Cup. We drew Manchester United at Old Trafford in the FA Cup third round, which was a massive draw and a dream for the club. We were top of the Championship, and at the time they were second in the Premiership. It was a great tie for the neutrals, but I was having a nightmare with injuries and was touch and go for match day. My ankle was playing up and I was having to take painkilling injections just to train once or twice a week. It was so bad that I missed a League game against Forest because I was in too much pain to play. The next match was the United game, and I knew deep down that I really wasn't fit enough to keep up with the likes of Giggs and Scholes, not in front of 70-odd thousand fans. But I also knew it was my last chance of playing a top-flight team like Man United in one of the world's greatest stadiums.

I was selfish. I thought, 'I'm coming to the end of my career, how many more times am I going to get a chance to play at Old Trafford? I'll be captain and lead the team out; the kids haven't been to Old Trafford before, so it will be a special day ...' I told Harry I was fit when really I should have been watching from the stands, and when I got on to the pitch I could hardly move. My ankle was shot and I couldn't get about the park. I was taken off at half-time and we were spanked 4-1.

Away from the game, I was just as fragile. A week on from the United defeat, I started to struggle with the gambling again. I went on another binge and I couldn't stop myself from ringing in bet after bet after bet. I don't know what had kick-started it all, but I was so desperate to stop the cycle of gambling that I went to Gamblers

How Not To Be a Professional Footballer

Anonymous for a while. I was sick of doing the same thing all the time, fed up with it. It was getting on my nerves.

But GA didn't help. I placed a £30,000 bet on one football match. Even though I lost, my first thought was to bet again – gambling kept spanking me big-time. I even told the papers about it, I was that desperate for help. Every day I considered suicide, the thought of ending it all was always there, because I was sick and tired of feeling sick and tired.

Harry was nothing but supportive, he was unbelievable. He wanted to get me help and told me he'd do everything he could to set me straight. I suppose he knew he was taking on a high-maintenance player when he signed me, but it was obvious to everyone that I needed a break. I noticed that there were a couple of gaps approaching on the fixture list, so I went into Harry's office on the morning of our next game to ask for some time off.

'Harry,' I said, 'we play this match today and then we haven't got a match for two weeks. I'm struggling with the gambling badly. I need to get into Tony Adams's treatment centre [the Sporting Chance Clinic, which Tone had opened in 2000], because I'm in that much trouble.'

He said, 'OK, Merse, I'll tell you what, son, play the game today and go into Tony's place and I'll see you a week on Monday.'

What a result. I got home after the game and told my missus, Louise, 'Pack your bags, we're going to Barbados tomorrow.'

Do Not Tell Harry Redknapp ...

I figured, 'Sod going to see Tone, I've got a week off, let's go on holiday.' I knew I could steer clear of the bookies if I was on the beach.

The next morning we got a flight out of England. I sat on the sand for a week and it was lovely, a million miles away from the rain and the cold of Portsmouth. There were even a few football fans milling about, so I had a good crack as we relaxed in the evenings. Then, a couple of days into the holiday, I bumped into a cockney bloke in the town as I was out picking up some Factor 1000 suncream. He wanted to stop for a chat.

'Hello, Merse, how are you? I'm Dave ...'

I just thought he was an England fan, so I began talking away.

'You're doing well down at Pompey, aren't you?' he said. 'Harry's got you going.'

I rabbited away for a good 20 minutes about this, that and the other, talking shop, and not once did this bloke let on that he was one of Harry's best mates. The minute I left him he went straight back to his villa and called the gaffer. Apparently, the conversation went something like this:

DAVE: All right, Harry, how's tricks?
HARRY: I'm good, Dave, what's happening, son?
DAVE: I've been with one of your lads this week ...
HARRY: Oh yeah, who's that?

DAVE: Merse, Paul Merson.

HARRY: Oh Dave, what's happened to you? You're not drinking heavily, are you? Please tell me it's not drugs. When did you check into Tony Adams's place?

DAVE: What are you on about, mate? I'm on holiday with the missus.

HARRY: Holiday? Where the bloody hell are you?

DAVE: Barbados.

HARRY: Effing Barbados?! The cheeky sod ...

The following Monday I turned up at the training ground for work as expected, completely unaware that I'd been caught out. Still, Harry didn't say a word and he would have had a cast-iron excuse to ask questions: my week in Barbados had given me a double tan; I was blacker than Shaka Hislop, our Trinidad & Tobago goalie. In fact Harry let it go, he didn't bring it up all season. It was only a year or so ago that he even told me that Dave had grassed me up. At the time he must have thought, 'Sod it, Merse is flying on the pitch for me and he's had a week or two off. I'll leave him alone.'

It worked. A break from the bookies seemed to get me back on track and Pompey kept on beating everyone in sight in the League. Harry's 10 frees and under-the-radar signings had turned into a cracking team. Svetoslav Todorov had signed a season earlier for £750,000 from West Ham and played up front, scoring 26 goals. He was joined by Nigerian striker Yakubu, who had originally come from the Israeli team Maccabi Haifa on loan before Harry signed him too. He seemed to score every other game in the Championship and was later sold to Boro for £7.5 million in 2005, which was a tidy bit of business for the club.

Tim Sherwood had a great season, but our best player was probably defender Linvoy Primus, who was phenomenal all year. He was a man mountain at the back. The funny thing was that Harry had originally only reckoned him to be a squad player at best. By Christmas, he was a regular in the side. We won the title by six points. I was getting my quarter mill bonus and Kev was getting his £10,000 housekeeping money. It was official: Pompey's kit man was running the most expensive laundry in the world. The tragic thing was, I was his best customer.

I didn't fancy it in the Premiership the following season. Harry wanted me to make more of a commitment to the team, which was fair enough, but that involved me moving down to Portsmouth. I wasn't too happy about that, and I didn't want to leave my wife and kids in the Midlands. I also realised that I'd found my standard in the Championship. It was perfect for me. Harry had given me a free role at Pompey, and I could just turn up and play anywhere on the park. I absolutely loved it, but I knew I'd be no good in the Premiership, where more discipline was needed, and the game was a million times faster. At my age it felt too much like hard work.

My decision to leave came at the last minute. I'd even been filmed for *Match of the Day*'s opening credits – I'd turned up in my kit and kicked the ball about for the BBC cameras. But Harry was as good as gold when I told him I couldn't hack it. He'd just signed former Spurs and United striker, Teddy Sheringham, another free, so he probably wasn't banking on using me as much as he had the previous season anyway.

'I'll tell you what, Merse,' he said. 'Go and get a club back home in the Midlands. I'll let you go on a free transfer and I'll get you some money.'

I was well chuffed. Another pay day meant I wouldn't feel so sick about giving Kev the kit man all that money, and at first I thought West Brom were going to sign me. Their chief exec had called. He reckoned I was on their list of potential summer signings and was I up for joining? Going to West Brom would mean I could stay in the Midlands. They'd just come down from the Premiership and were a top club with top players. They were also one of the favourites to go up, so I reckoned I could have a season as good as the one I'd had with Harry.

I asked about the manager, Gary Megson. 'Is he happy with you talking to me?'

There was a pause. 'We haven't talked to Gary yet.'

I laughed. 'What? That's no good. He's got to want me or there's no point.'

I knew I wasn't Gary's kind of player. I wasn't the type to kick balls towards corner flags, I wanted to spray passes around. I'm not being horrible, but his teams didn't play the style of football I was used to. I told them I knew that Gary wouldn't fancy me.

'We want you,' came the reply. 'He's on holiday, so we'll contact him there and it'll all be sorted.' I wasn't convinced.

Three days later, West Brom called me back.

'You're fucking right, Merse,' they said. 'He don't want you.'

The only club that wanted me after that were Walsall. Their manager, Colin Lee, came over to sign me and they offered a good wage, so I went for it. Like West Brom, they were a Championship side, so trust the two teams to meet on my debut. I bumped into Gary Megson before the game and everything was fine – we had a laugh. I told him there were no hard feelings.

That day, the Bescott Stadium was packed out, it was a local derby and it was a scorching hot August after-noon, about 1,000 degrees. Judging by the atmosphere, we were already playing a cup final at the start of the season. But what a day. We won 4–1, I got two and Walsall went top of the table for the first time in the club's history.

How Not To Be a Professional Footballer

The following morning, the papers were writing silly stories. One headline even screamed: 'The Messiah Is Back!' A writer was banging on about how I was going to be the saviour of Walsall. I ignored it. The last thing I needed was to get carried away with a win and a couple of goals, because inside I was losing the plot. Louise had just left me. She'd had enough of my recurring gambling habit. In an attempt to block out the pain I'd made a £60,000 flutter and I was back on another gambling streak. When it didn't come in, I was in ruins. I checked my bank account the next day and I could see I was rapidly throwing away every last penny I'd earned with Villa and Pompey, but I was on self-destruct mode. It was only going to get worse.

It was me that needed the saviour, not Walsall.

Do Not Smile at a Sex Addict Called Candy

'Out of the frying pan and into the fire:
A gambling binge sends Merse over the edge.
Then he becomes the manager of Walsall.'

I was gone. My life was in bits. It was a season or so into my new career at Walsall when the wife divorced me, February 2004. My second marriage was down the toilet, the kids had left, and I'd lost my house. I was living in a small flat around the corner from the Bescott Stadium, so I wasn't exactly skipping into work every morning. My old mates, booze and betting, were back again, but as one beer led to a lorryload more, the absolutely worst thing in the world that could have happened to me at that moment happened: I turned 35.

How Not To Be a Professional Footballer

On paper, this isn't the most disastrous landmark in the world, but at 35 professional footballers can draw on their pension. Sure, they can leave it in there and watch the money go up and up and up until they're 65, but some people want to take it all out in one lump. I was one of those people. I drew out all £800,000 of it in one hit and blew it in a couple of months. I went betting crazy.

I placed some silly wagers. Sixty grand here, eighty grand there. My system was all over the place and I was gambling on absolutely anything and everything. Every morning when I went to training, the players would meet up at the Bescott Stadium and change, then we'd be driven to a local school. Because we didn't have a training ground we'd play on their pitches for the morning. Often we'd often have to hang around while the kids finished hockey practice or whatever. While I was sitting there, I'd ring up a bookie and bet £10,000 on something like who would be the first batsman out at Lord's that day. I was that off my head.

Because of the amounts I was spending, I couldn't keep my gambling a secret for long. Shortly after my disastrous cricket bets, I went down to the newsagent to get a Sunday paper and got the shock of my life when I saw that my face was plastered over the back page of the *News of the World*. They'd got to hear about my binge and had written a big story on me. Even worse, they'd listed all my bets.

Do Not Smile at a Sex Addict Called Candy

£10,000 on the first one out at Lord's.

£15,000 on Holland getting the first corner against Scotland.

£15,000 on Federer to win one afternoon …

The list went on and on and on. A journalist had managed to get all my payments, something that was supposed to be confidential information. I rang up my bookies, furious.

'My God, what's happened?' I shouted at the bloke on the other end of the line. 'I bet with you because of the confidentiality. I could get booted out of Walsall tomorrow because of this.'

The bloke was tripping over himself to apologise. 'I'm so sorry,' he said. 'This has been an inside job. Somebody rang up from the press and somehow they've got into your details. Look, we've had a meeting. We're going to give back what you lost last month.'

Result. 'How much is that then?'

'Oh, it's £90,000,' he said.

I practically bit his hand off, but I was mad really. If I'd sued the company I probably would have got a quarter mill in my back pocket in compensation, but I was just happy to claw back some of my money I'd lost. It meant I could gamble and gamble some more until every last penny had gone.

I knew I was in trouble; the newspaper story was a warning. I'd wasted my pension away to nothing. In spite of everything I'd done in the game – winning titles at Arsenal, playing in World Cups, scoring for England – I'd lost my wife, kids, house and all my money. I went to see the Walsall chairman, Jeff Bonser, for help because I was in pieces and potless. I was done in. For the second time in my life I was dropping another scandal on a club board, but Jeff was just as sympathetic as the chairman and directors of Arsenal had been in 1994.

'We need to get you help, son,' he said.

He got me in front of the Professional Footballers' Association, who tried to work out a way of setting me straight.

'Right, we need to get you into a treatment centre,' they said. 'There's a place in Arizona called Sierra Tucson. It's phenomenal, but it costs £20,000 a month to go there.'

I knew I couldn't afford that. I didn't have £20 in my pocket, let alone £20,000, but the PFA had a plan.

'The club are going to keep you, despite this mess,' they said. 'They'll loan you the money and you can pay them back with money out of your wages.'

I agreed, but I had no option really. I would have taken anything to stop the gambling. I was flown over with Jim Walker, my old physio from Villa, because the PFA wanted to make sure I had checked in. They didn't want me doing a runner, and they were probably being sensible. As the plane flew over Arizona I really couldn't face staying away

Do Not Smile at a Sex Addict Called Candy

from England for a whole month. It felt like years. The treatment centre was in the middle of nowhere. There was nothing there but the building itself and sand, cactus and dust.

Inside it was a top place. I could see mountains from my bedroom window, the rooms were comfy, and the whole building felt peaceful and calm. It was just about the best place a compulsive gambler with a history of drink and drugs could be in.

On my first morning I got up at 6 a.m. and had my breakfast, which was eggs, sausage, orange juice, the works. It felt like I was staying in a top-drawer hotel. Then I learnt I was eating 15 minutes later than the people with eating disorders, because they needed special help with their food.

After breakfast we were called into my first group session. It was being held in a special meeting room, and all the chairs had been arranged in a neat square so everyone could see one another. To be honest, I thought I was staring at the pages of a celebrity magazine. I recognised pretty much everyone in the group, because they were all double famous. I'm not going to name names, but I was sitting with actresses, Oscar winners, NFL stars, basketball players and singers. It blew my mind.

A counsellor came in and told us our first task was to introduce ourselves to one another.

How Not To Be a Professional Footballer

'Hi, I'm Famous Hollywood Star What'sname,' said the first bloke. 'I'm in treatment for an addiction to painkillers ...'

The next: 'Hi, I'm Celebrity NBA What'sname. I can't stop drinking ...'

It went on and on. As this was happening, I noticed the fittest girl I'd ever seen in my life sitting opposite me. Oh my God, she was beautiful. Long blonde hair, pretty face, knockout body. She caught me eyeing her up and smiled. Then she winked and licked her lips like she'd been eating the best-tasting ice cream in the world. I couldn't believe it. I had to look over my shoulder to make sure that there wasn't a hunky Hollywood actor sitting behind me. It would have been so embarrassing if her sexy looks had been aimed at him, but there was no one there.

'Bingo,' I thought. 'Whatever happens, I'm getting my £20,000 worth.'

Then it was my turn to introduce myself to the group.

'All right, I'm Paul. I'm a professional footballer from England. I have a gambling problem.'

I waited for the turn of the Sexy What'sname opposite. I fantasised in my head about who and what she was. She could quite easily have been model or a pop star. Maybe even a former Miss America? When it came to her turn to say hello, she looked me straight in the eye.

'Hi, everyone,' she said in a sexy Californian drawl. 'My name's Candy and I'm a sex addict.'

Do Not Smile at a Sex Addict Called Candy

My heart sank. She was winking at me because she couldn't help herself. Sure enough, it turned out that every bloke in the room had been given an eyeful during the meeting – I was just one of a dozen. At the end of my stay in Sierra Tucson I found out that a janitor had managed to bed her.

I worked there for a month, talking through my problems, trying to discover the root of my gambling issues. I thought we had done pretty well by the time my four weeks were up. I was ready to go home; I thought I could get my life back on track at Walsall, no problems. My therapist had other ideas. The day before I was due to fly back, I was called into her office.

'Paul, you're due to go home tomorrow,' she said. 'But I think you should stay here for another nine months. You are without doubt the worst pathological gambler we've ever had come through here.'

I didn't have a clue what that meant. I told her I was going home.

'How can I stay here?' I said. 'I miss my kids. The football team miss me.'

I knew the second part was a lie. I'd been playing so badly during my gambling spell that the lads probably hadn't noticed that I'd even left. In my defence, I was knackered most of the time. Walsall had some good players, like the former Spurs midfielder Vinny Samways, but we were getting beaten too often and a lot of the lads didn't like it that I didn't train as much as them.

When I signed, I told the manager, Colin Lee, 'I don't work Mondays, I don't work Wednesdays and I don't work Fridays. I'll play Saturday. I played 50-odd games last year like that and it worked.'

At first they were happy with the arrangement, but then one or two of the lads started to complain. Colin made me work all week, and by Saturday I was knackered. I couldn't play and my form went pear-shaped. Despite this, I was desperate to fly home and play sooner rather than later.

There was also the financial side to consider. Staying in treatment was going to cost me an arm and a leg. I told my counsellor that I'd already spent £20,000 that I didn't have on a month of treatment. There was no way I could afford another £180,000, but she wasn't giving up on me that easily.

'Paul, there's an apartment up the road you can rent from us,' she said. 'We've got you a job in the local super-market, packing bags. You can earn money there all day and pay rent, then you can come and see us in the evening. We advise you to stay, because you really aren't well.'

I wasn't having it. I flew out of Arizona the next morning. Not even 24 hours after I'd left, Gazza flew in to Sierra Tucson. For weeks he'd been waiting to come in for treatment, but the doctors refused to treat the pair of us at the same time. They reckoned we'd cause too much trouble together. The driver who took me to the airport would later meet Gaz and drive him to the centre. One in, one out. It was like the 1998 World Cup all over again.

I must have looked pretty healthy when I got back from the States, because only a couple of months after my return, Jeff Bonser made me the manager of the club. Walsall had not had the best of seasons, and by March we were fifth from bottom of the division. Our next game was against Norwich City, who were top of the table and battering everyone in sight. On the morning of the game we all arrived at the ground, but by 10.30 the gaffer, Colin Lee, hadn't arrived for work. An hour later he still wasn't there.

The lads were hanging round the players' lounge when I received a message to visit the chairman's office. Once I got there, I was told to sit down. I'd been around the block enough to know that this was one of those serious meetings that sometimes take place between club owner and senior player.

'I've just sacked Colin,' said Jeff. 'He was talking to Plymouth. His heart wasn't in it.'

I was surprised, but not shocked. Nothing shocked me in football any more. 'So what are you going to do?'

He looked at me from across his desk. 'I'm going to put you in charge.'

How Not To Be a Professional Footballer

I couldn't believe it. 'But Mr Chairman, I can't even look after myself, let alone a Championship football team.'

He didn't care. Whether I liked it or not I was the new Walsall gaffer.

Talk about a baptism of fire. After two minutes we were 1-0 down to Norwich. After 90 we'd been walloped by five, but that was just the beginning. I was put in charge for the last three games of the season, and Walsall were in the middle of a relegation dogfight. It wasn't going well. In the penultimate game we lost to Palace with the last kick of the match, setting up a do-or-die game with Rotherham. At the same time, we needed Stoke to beat Gillingham at their place, which looked possible, because Stoke were double good at home. That weekend we won 3-2, but Gillingham held Stoke to a goalless draw and we were relegated on goal difference. It wasn't a nice feeling.

I'd enjoyed managing, though. From the age of about 28 I'd always fancied having a go at it. Maybe Arsène Wenger had turned me on to it in the same way as he got Bouldy and Tone interested. But I think it was more to do with the fact that I didn't know anything else other than football, and I knew that I couldn't play for the rest of my life. Management was an obvious step forward for me, especially as I didn't have a fat pension to live off any more.

Walsall was a great start for a young gaffer like myself. They were a good little club and they weren't going to go belly up financially, because they were well run. Jeff had obviously seen some promise in me, because he wanted me to stay on into the new season. I was given the same wage packet as I'd been on as a player (minus the repayments for Sierra Tucson, of course), which was a lot of money for them, especially as we'd been relegated.

I couldn't believe how hard managing a football club was. As a player, everything was done for me. As a manager I was the one who had to make sure everything got done. It also didn't help that I'd been quite high maintenance as a footballer. My managers would all say that I was hard work during the week because I always had a million problems, and if I didn't like training, I would catch the ball halfway through a practice game and boot it down the road because I had the hump about something.

Now this group of lads, the same ones who laughed as I mucked Colin Lee about, had to take orders from me. As a manager I was easy. The players could have their mobiles in the dressing-room as long as they weren't using them when I was talking, but one of two of them took the piss. In pre-season, at a weekend, one of the lads called me up while I was having a barbecue. He wanted to tell me he'd been done for drink-driving.

I said, 'Yeah? What the fuck are you telling me now for? I'm with the family, I'm having a barbecue. Don't ring me now. Talk to me Monday.'

How Not To Be a Professional Footballer

We had the makings of a good side at Walsall, and I liked working with the players. We had Matty Fryatt, who would go to play for Leicester and Hull City. Daniel Fox had nice moves to Burnley and Celtic after Walsall. Scott Dann was in defence, and he later went on to play for Birmingham City. At the time, though, I never thought he had a hope in hell of making it. I once sent him out on loan to Redditch and they sent him back because he couldn't cut it even at their level, and they were four or five leagues below us. He was no good. I saw him recently at the pictures and I was pleased to see him. I couldn't believe that he'd made a bit of a hit in the Premier League.

'You proved me wrong, mate,' I said.

I liked working with the managers, too. Alex Ferguson often called me up because we had one of his lads, Mads Timm, on loan. When he was at training I thought he was the best player ever, but when it came to Saturday he couldn't turn it on. If I could have got our kick-offs changed to 10.30 on a Tuesday morning I'd have got him an international call-up, he played that well in practice games. Fergie would ring up to chat about him, and even though there wasn't much to report, we'd always have a chinwag for half an hour or so. Mick McCarthy was the same; there was a real support network among gaffers. I loved it.

I'd learnt from my old managers as well. I wrote down loads of Wenger stuff in a notebook when I worked with him at Arsenal; I used all sorts of drills that he'd first used on us when I became manager of Walsall. It didn't really work, though. A crucial difference between Arsène and me was that he had top-drawer players to work with like Dennis, Thierry Henry and Tone. Not me. It didn't matter what I'd injected into my lads at Walsall or how I'd got them to stretch, it was the fact that they couldn't play that often lost me games.

My biggest problem was dealing with the financial side of the game. Walsall weren't exactly loaded with cash, and the chairman often had to spend money to balance the books, especially after the TV company ITV Digital went into administration in 2002, which meant a lot of football clubs lost their telly money. I had to sell a lot of players, but I couldn't moan. I was grateful to have a manager's job, and I wasn't in a position to walk because I didn't have any money myself.

We managed to stay up in 2004–05, but it was close. On transfer deadline day I was allowed to bring in some players, including the former Villa striker Julian Joachim and Steven Gerrard's cousin, Anthony. We even went through all of April unbeaten, but I still had to sell. I took all the chairman's demands on the chin, but deep down I knew I couldn't make Walsall a success if we were going to have to flog all our best players. We struggled for the rest of the year.

How Not To Be a Professional Footballer

From the minute I got the job, the fans had been split against me. Some of them loved me, some of them hated me, and there were always rumours that I was going to get the boot. When Leicester City came in for striker Matty Fryatt in January 2006 there was nothing I could do to stop the club from selling. He was our best player at the time. As you can imagine, the supporters weren't exactly happy to see him go.

We were a dog and duck team. At home we were capable of getting a result, but on the road we were a nightmare, and that's what ultimately got me the tin tack. After we'd beaten Barnsley in the 2005-06 FA Cup we had to play a lot of away games in quick succession, and I had a horrible feeling that it was a run that might cost me my job. I even told the press. They asked me what I thought of the Barnsley game and Walsall's hopes for the rest of the season.

'It was a great result,' I said. 'The lads played really well. It was a pleasure. But that result could get me the sack.'

Everyone started laughing, but I knew it was true. We'd drawn Stoke away in the next round, which meant we weren't going to be playing at home for ages. Sure enough, we didn't win for four games, which included a 2-1 defeat in the FA Cup. In a relegation scrap against Swindon Town we lost 1-0, and against Brentford it was even worse.

Do Not Smile at a Sex Addict Called Candy

Brentford were the last team we wanted to play. Martin Allen was the manager and they were flying. We lost 5-0, and in the opening attack by Brentford our goalie, Andy Oakes, got injured and had to come off. A couple of minutes later, one of their strikers rounded our reserve keeper and rolled the ball into the net. Before it had even trickled across the line, two idiots behind the goal had hung up a banner with the words 'MERSON OUT' painted on it. I knew right then the writing was on the wall.

I hammered a few of the lads in the dressing-room after the game, and when I walked out, the chairman was waiting for me for a chat.

'Mr Chairman, this is no good,' I said. 'We're fifth from bottom. I resign. I've taken this as far as I can and I don't need fans calling me every name under the sun, especially not when my kids are in the ground.'

Jeff calmed me down. 'Don't be silly,' he said. 'Come in on Monday. We've got Scunthorpe at home next week. We're good at home. We'll bring some players in on loan and we'll get a result at the weekend.'

He was desperate to help me. On Monday after training we sat down as promised and talked through some potential signings, and then I went off to get my hair cut in Toni and Guy, because a mate of mine worked there. As he was snipping away, my phone rang. It was Walsall's chief exec, Roy Whalley.

'Merse, I need to talk to you,' he said.

'Sure thing, Roy, how about I come in early tomorrow at eight-thirty?'

'No,' he said. 'I need to speak to you now.'

I arranged to meet him later that night, and I didn't think anything of it, but my mate started winding me up.

'He's probably going to sack you.'

'Shut up,' I said. 'They're not sacking me. They've just talked me out of resigning.'

When I got to the club, Roy looked pretty serious. 'We've got a problem,' he said. 'There's going to be a bit of a riot on Saturday. The fans really aren't happy.'

I said, 'What do you mean, a riot? We've got Scunthorpe. Their supporters will probably come down on one motorbike.'

Roy shook his head. 'Not their fans, our fans. They're not happy. I think you should resign.'

I wasn't having it. I told him there was no way I was jacking it in now. 'If you want to get rid, you'll have to sack me.'

Roy shrugged his shoulders. 'All right then, you're sacked.'

I was gutted. Any dreams I had of carving out a career for myself in management were over. It was a bit harsh, but I could hardly argue. Football management is a results business, and Walsall's results had been bloody awful.

LESSON 18

Do Not Try to Outwit Jeff Stelling

'Merse joins the Soccer Saturday crew with Jeff Stelling and The Crazy Gang. TV chaos ensues.'

My last ever game in competitive football was a bloody 'mare. In February 2006 I got snapped up by Tamworth, another Midlands club, on a part-time playing contract. They were in the Conference and an old mate of mine, Mark Cooper, was the manager, but signing for them turned out to be a right ricket. I hadn't played for ages. At Walsall I'd been involved in training, but not enough to keep up my match fitness. I should have played more games at Walsall, because our record was good when I started, but I wanted to concentrate on the management side more than the playing. That was a mistake.

I made my Tamworth debut against Halifax in the Conference, but I was useless, the worst player on the pitch. Crap. I couldn't keep up with the pace of the game and it was physically tougher than I'd ever imagined. Those leagues didn't get enough credit when I was a player; thinking about it, there's not much difference between the Conference and the Championship. A lot of the teams down there would give anyone a game.

The following week we trained on a Tuesday night, but I wanted to watch the Chelsea-Barcelona game that was being shown on the telly. It was chucking it down, and halfway through a practice game, I'd had enough. I walked off towards the clubhouse.

'Where are you going?' said Mark.

'This is wrong,' I said. 'We should be in there watching Chelsea-Barca, not playing out here.'

Mark took it quite well, but when it came to the next game, which was against Grays the following Saturday, he mucked me about. I'd met the team on the coach as it pulled into a service station on the M6. I'd been waiting there for ages, so I had the hump anyway, but as I sat down, Mark leant across to me.

'I'm going to leave you out today, Merse. You're sub,' he said. 'We've got a big game in the week at home and I want you to be fresh.'

I thought he was taking the piss. 'You what? I could have stayed at home and watched *Soccer Saturday*. Why bring me if you knew you weren't starting me?'

Do Not Try to Outwit Jeff Stelling

I sat there for the rest of the journey like a little kid. When I got to the ground, I got changed into my tracksuit and walked round the pitch to the bench. As I passed the fans, some of them started calling out to me.

'Merse, why aren't you playing? We've come to watch you play.'

I pointed over to the dugout. 'You should ask that prick there,' I shouted.

Mark was my mate, but I was fed up. I sat behind him on the bench, staring into the back of his head. Well, it was better than watching the football. After 10 minutes we were 1–0 down. After 12 we had a man sent off. Then we conceded another goal with only quarter of an hour played. It was a shambles. Mark turned round to me. I could tell he wanted to bring me on.

'Don't even think about,' I snarled. 'Do not even think about it.'

We lost 5–0, and at the end of the game I walked into the dressing-room. Mark was still talking to the team but I ignored him and put my clothes on, I didn't even have a shower. Nicky Summerbee, the former Man City midfielder, was a sub as well and he'd brought his car with him.

'Do us a favour, give me a lift home, mate,' I said.

We walked out of the ground with the fans. I never kicked a football in anger again.

How Not To Be a Professional Footballer

I knew my football career was over, but the strange thing was, I didn't feel too bad. When I was younger I thought football was never going to end for me. I figured I would be playing for ever. Retirement seemed such a long way away when I was a kid that I couldn't imagine doing anything else with my life, but as I got nearer to the last days of my playing career I wasn't that bothered about hanging up my boots. I'd got fed up with being given the runaround by kids who wouldn't have got near me if they'd been playing 10 years earlier. And I didn't need fans getting on my back at the age of 38. Do me a favour. The only thing I lost when I walked out on Tamworth was the 30 minutes of laughing around with the other lads before kick-off and the 30 minutes after a game or training. Ask any retired professional footballer: the part of the job that ex-players miss more than anything is the banter.

Then I got a call that would change my Saturday afternoons for the better. Several months after that game at Grays, Sky called me up out of the blue and asked if I wanted to be a panellist for their results show, *Soccer Saturday*. I was up for it, because I knew that joining the panel was a good way of keeping in touch with the laughs, and I really didn't fancy getting up on a Saturday morning and having nothing to do except sit in front of the telly (watching *Soccer Saturday*). Instead, I wanted to be *on* the telly.

Do Not Try to Outwit Jeff Stelling

My only problem was that I knew nothing about working in the media. I had no qualifications and no TV experience. I learnt sod all at school and my only specialist subjects were football and betting, and I wasn't very good at either of those at the time. I couldn't talk in *Countdown* Conundrums like Tone, and I wasn't well spoken like Graeme Le Saux or Gary Lineker, so I didn't think I'd have much of a chance, but they still wanted me to come on the show anyway.

I could see the appeal of having me there. It turned out that *Soccer Saturday* had become a bit of a retirement home for some of football's biggest bad boys and characters. Charlie Nicholas was on the panel, and he'd hardly been squeaky clean in his time. George Best had been a popular pundit before he died of alcohol-related problems in 2005, and he was one of the biggest playboys and boozers around.

I admit it, going on *Soccer Saturday* was a dream come true for me. If somebody had asked me to plan my ideal week as a Walsall player, I would have said, 'Mate, I'll take a Sunday or Monday night kick-off, train on Saturday morning, go to the bookies after and put my bets on, then I'll watch *Soccer Saturday* all afternoon, thank you very much.' I loved the show, I was like a fan. I'd have my betting slips in front of me on the coffee table and I'd watch the lads talking about the games as the scores came in. It was bliss.

How Not To Be a Professional Footballer

Not everyone gets the appeal of the show, but usually they're people who don't know about football. I can understand the confusion, though. On paper, *Soccer Saturday* sounds crazy, especially to someone who's never seen it. Basically, four ex-professional footballers – Charlie, Southampton legend Matt Le Tissier, Liverpool trophy hunter Phil Thompson and me – sit in front of TV screens in a live studio. After three hours of discussing all the football news and form guides, we watch games on the tellies in front of us and relay the info and action to an audience of millions (you can't show live football on a Saturday afternoon). Organising all the chaos and drama is presenter and statto Jeff Stelling, as the rest of us yell our heads off at goals, sendings-off, Drogba dives and dodgy offside decisions. It looks like a right nuthouse.

Whoever went into the head office at Sky with the idea for the show must have had been more off his head than me at the time. Can you imagine it? 'All right, Boss,' he says. 'I've got this brilliant idea for a football results programme. Right, there's no footy to see, but I'll get four blokes to watch the games and scream and shout as the goals go in. What do you reckon?'

Sky bloke: 'Yeah right, mate. Nurse!'

It must seem even crazier to people who don't understand the game as they flick on the telly and catch the programme. I bet a lorryload of arguments have started with *Soccer Saturday*: a football fan watches the show at

Do Not Try to Outwit Jeff Stelling

home and his partner watches him – watching us watching football – jaw on the floor, thinking, 'What the bloody hell are you doing?'

I was just as confused when I sat behind the desk for the first time. I made my debut on Sky Sports' *Soccer Special*, which is the weekday version of *Soccer Saturday*, with presenter Rob McCaffrey. Jeff wasn't there to guide me through the programme, but I had plenty of help on the night because former Villa and Bayern Munich headbanger Alan McInally sat on one side of me, and Charlie was on the other. Between them they talked me through the rules as I settled into the studio dressing-rooms and got my make-up done.

Once I was there at the large desk in the middle of the studio, the cameras rolling, I was like a pig in shit. I had my headphones on, the football was on the telly and loads of betting slips were placed in front of me, because I'd been in the bookies all afternoon. It was like being at home on a Saturday. A lot was riding on the games that night, too. Well, for me anyway.

My job was to cover Hull's game against Barnsley, a Championship fixture which would turn out to be a right 'mare, mainly because there wasn't any commentary coming through my headphones. At first I thought they were knackered.

'I can't hear anything, Rob,' I moaned in the first ad break. 'Have my headphones gone pear?'

'No, Merse,' he said. 'It's a Championship game and we haven't got any commentators working there tonight. You'll have to go without.'

'Bloody hell,' I thought. 'I'm in shit here, because I don't know any of these players from fucking Adam.'

It was to get worse. There were no action replays in my game either. If something dramatic happened, I'd have to watch the game like a hawk so I could catch the names that were printed on the players' shirts. I also had to memorise everything: bookings, free-kicks, offsides and shots on target which was double hard. I was freaking out – talk about a baptism of fire.

These days it's different, because I'm usually doing a Premier League game on *Soccer Saturday*. I can relax, because the bigger matches come with commentary, replays, slow motion, the lot. I can watch Arsenal playing Bolton over Phil Thompson's shoulder on the other telly, and if I miss something in my game, I can catch the action replay later on. It's a doddle.

Hull versus Barnsley that night was a horror show. The pictures were a blur – it looked as if somebody was filming the game from a mobile phone. The only player I knew on the pitch was Dean Windass. I guessed straight away he was going to have a worldy game because Windass was the only person I'd be able to talk about with any authority, but after 15 minutes I'd bluffed my way through a couple of reports and felt quite relaxed.

Do Not Try to Outwit Jeff Stelling

That's when I got into trouble. On the big screen behind the camera crew in the studio is a plasma screen telly which shows the vidiprinter. Viewers can see it at the bottom of their screens whenever they flick on to the programme, but there's a giant version for us. As the scores started to flash up at half-time, I began checking them against my betting slips.

Wolves had scored.

'I've got them,' I thought. 'Blinding.'

Crystal Palace were one up.

'I've got them too, I'm flying.'

Leicester were winning 2–0.

'Get in there!'

I couldn't keep my eyes off the vidiprinter. That addictive and compulsive personality of mine was in overdrive, so by the time the second half had got underway, I was wasn't paying a blind bit of attention to Hull versus Barnsley, I was checking up on my bets. The only result I was unsure of was Crewe. I knew that if they won that night, I'd be going home with a fortune.

I turned round to McInally. 'What's the Crewe score?' I whispered in his ear.

He shrugged his shoulders. 'I dunno, I think it might be 2–1 to them.'

'What do you mean?' I hissed. 'I'm waiting on that one to win a fortune. What's the bloody score?'

How Not To Be a Professional Footballer

I started checking the vidiprinter, searching for the words 'Crewe' and 'Alexandra'. I was rustling my betting slips nervously on the desk. Then my heart dropped into my stomach. At the bottom of the page, in big red letters, the vidiprinter was flashing: 'SENDING OFF, ASHBY (HULL).'

Oh shit. I stared down at my screen. This Ashby geezer was storming off the pitch in a right mood, kicking the grass. I thought, 'Oh my God, please show it again, please show it again, please show it again.' But I was waiting for an action replay that was never going to arrive. I was screwed.

'So, there's been a sending off in the Hull versus Barnsley game,' shouted Rob McCaffrey.

I started shaking my head and mouthing the word 'No!' at him from across the desk. Rob couldn't give a monkey's – he probably thought I was suffering from stage fright.

'Over to the KC Stadium and Paul Merson.'

Bollocks, I'd been busted. I looked down at my screen for clues, but I was like a fish up a tree.

'I dunno, Rob,' I said. 'I didn't see it.'

Rob looked at me open-mouthed. McInally started kicking me underneath the desk.

'Make it up, you prick,' he said.

But I was done for. I couldn't 'fess up or explain to Rob and the audience that I'd been checking my bets, or that

Do Not Try to Outwit Jeff Stelling

Crewe were in line to win me a fortune. Not after all the headlines that had been written about me and my gambling problems. That would have dropped me into some serious hot water. Rob shrugged his shoulders and made a gag out of it; I was given a bit of a ticking off after the show had ended. Honestly, I thought I'd blown it, big-time, but miraculously I was asked back again. Somehow, Hull's loss had been my gain.

Jeff Stelling and the lads are so good at what they do in the studio, it's scary. When I walked into the Sky offices for the first time I didn't really have a clue what was going on, I felt way out of my depth. But when I watched the professionals at work, they made the results game look so simple, especially Jeff.

I honestly can't believe the amount of knowledge he's memorised. Sure, if a goal comes in from Queen of the South and he starts banging on about how it's 'What'sname's third of the season!' that's because he's got someone shouting the stats in his ear. But for the Premier League, Championship, or Leagues One and Two, it's all in his head.

My only problem with the show is that it plays havoc with my waistline. We don't stop eating from the minute we sit down behind the desk. When we start work at 12, the crew give us soup, which would normally be enough for me. But then, at one, the omelettes come round; and me and Le Tiss will always get some chips to munch on between courses. I'll have a bag of crisps during an ad break, some Red Bull, a Yorkie bar, maybe a bag of Revels. I said to my girlfriend once, 'If they put all the snacks we eat during one afternoon in a bucket, I would never eat it. It would look like such a disgusting amount of food, but I just can't stop stuffing my face.'

I even ate a Bounty bar once, just for the sake of it. I never eat Bounty bars, they're bloody horrible.

There is one thing I have to be on my guard about all the time while I'm working on the show – because I have a problem pronouncing the players' names. Like I said before, I never learnt a lot at school. All I understood as a kid was football. I wasn't one for grammar, Shakespeare or elocution. That was fine when I was sitting in the dressing-rooms at Arsenal, Villa, Boro or Pompey, but on the *Soccer Saturday* panel I'm always getting stick for the way I pronounce the names of some of football's biggest foreign players.

The thing is, I'm dyslexic and often get the tricky names jumbled up when I say them live on air. Most of the time I have the teamsheets in front of me, written down phonetically (Jeff taught me that word), which helps, but oh my God, when the Russian striker Diniyar Bilyaletdinov signed for Everton in 2009 I thought my Sky career was dead in the water. It's not just the eastern European footballers with *Countdown* Conundrum surnames that get me in a mess. I even struggle to get my head around the name of the Wolves striker Sylvan Ebanks-Blake, and he was born in Cambridge. Funnily enough, he lives near me, and when he clocked me in our local Waitrose the other month he started laughing in the fruit and veg aisle.

'You still can't nail it, can you?' he said. 'My mum rang me up and was going on about you, moaning, "That Merse bloke always gets your name wrong on TV. What's up with him?"'

I just wish Mrs Ebanks-Blake had called her son Steven. There wouldn't have been a problem. Not in a million years.

I'm not usually a great judge of people, and sometimes when I meet new pundits for the first time, I might think, 'Hmm, I'm not really having him.' Most of the time I'm wrong. Neil Warnock is the greatest example, because when he's screaming and shouting from the touchlines, he's an absolute horror show. Oh my God, I've been playing when he's been the opposition manager and he's yelled at his defenders to get me.

'Do him! Do him!' he'd shout.

He'd try anything to win a game of football, but off the pitch he's the loveliest bloke you could meet.

How Not To Be a Professional Footballer

The panel are great as well. I've known Charlie since I was a kid. It's funny, he took me under his wing at Arsenal and he did the same at Sky. I love the bloke (though we don't go to Stringfellows any more). When he was 23 years old at Arsenal, he was a handful, but he's completely turned his life around – he's a real family man now. Matt Le Tissier was one of the most talented footballers I'd ever seen when I was a player. It's just a shame he didn't get more caps. I'd have loved to see him play for a big, big team.

Then there's Thommo, another legend. He won just about everything with Liverpool, but punters are divided about him. They'll always say, 'What's that big nose, Thompson, like?' The truth is, he's blinding. You couldn't meet a nicer person and he's a real supporter. When Liverpool lose, he is absolutely devastated.

It's the players we talk about that do my head in. Honestly, they seem to care so much about what we say about them on the telly, that every little criticism gets blown out of proportion. I've only got to open my mouth for somebody to slag me off on Twitter. A couple of years ago I did an after-dinner speech at Sunderland and all the players were there, having a laugh. Weeks before I'd hammered Keiran Richardson on the show because he hadn't been playing that well. When I walked past him he looked at me like I was a piece of shit. It did my head in. For a little while I'd duck into my coat collars every time I saw a player at the driving range or in the supermarket.

'Bloody hell,' I'd think. 'Did I slate him last week? Is he going to have the hump with me?'

I've got used to it now, but it still happens. At the start of 2011, when Liverpool had been having a rough time and Roy Hodgson left the club, I had a pop at Liverpool full-back Glen Johnson which blew up big-time. Johnson had come up in conversation during *Soccer Saturday* and I made the point that he was great going forward – one of the best, in fact – but I also mentioned that he hadn't been playing well. Johnson must have been sitting there watching the show, because by the time I'd gone off air he'd shot his mouth off on Twitter.

'Comments from alcoholic drug abusers are not really gonna upset me,' he wrote. 'And who is Paul Merson to judge players? He was average at the best of times. The only reason he's on that show is coz he gambled all his money away. The clown!'

Obviously I'd touched a nerve. Funny, I don't remember Johnson Twittering me when I described him as one of the best attack-minded full-backs around before the last World Cup. The same thing happened with Frank Lampard: I said some nice things about him one season and nothing happened. The minute I criticised one of his performances, he got the hump. His agent called me up. 'Frank ain't happy with what you said,' he reckoned.

How Not To Be a Professional Footballer

Glen Johnson is entitled to think what he likes about me. I know I divide opinion. Half the time people love me, the other half they hate me, and that's fine. I will always speak my mind. If someone's not very good, I'll say so. If they then start playing worldies every week, then I'll put my hands up and apologise. So if Glen Johnson sets the world alight in the next year I'll be the first person to congratulate him, but why would he care? He reckons that my winning two League titles, an FA Cup, the League Cup and a UEFA Cup Winner's Cup makes me an 'average at best' player. He must have had a much better career than the rest of the world realises.

LESSON
19

Do Not Admit Defeat (the Day-to-Day Battle)

'Merse talks about the here and now ...'

People always ask me whether I would have lived my life in the same way had I not been a football player. The answer is probably yes, but I'd have got into a lorryload more trouble. I would have had to beg, borrow and steal to gamble; I'd have been in the gutter with the booze. I don't even want to imagine what could have happened on drugs.

I got a small look into what might have been when I was in rehab in 1994. A bloke got up in front of the group in our Narcotics Anonymous meeting. It was his turn to do the Step One presentation, the point in his treatment where he had to tell everyone his life story. He told the group that he'd started out on coke, before moving on to heroin and crack. He'd come close to killing himself and along the way he lost everything – his family, his job and his life. When he spoke, he seemed like a normal fella, just like me, but he'd nearly done himself in on drugs.

I could tell that I had a similar personality to that bloke and that, like him, cocaine probably wouldn't have been enough to satisfy me after a while. As the buzz of coke got boring or wore off, I would have wanted something more, like heroin. God knows where that would have left me. In the same state as him most probably. Chances are I wouldn't be here today – I'd be six feet under.

Because everyone knows what I got up to when I was a player, I get the same questions whenever I'm out and about:

Why did you do what you did?

Why did you piss it up a wall?

Why did you drink and drive?

Why did you blow £7 million in the bookies?

Why did you snort all that coke?

It would be too easy to blame it all on the money I earned as a footballer; and it wasn't anything to do with the fact that I had all the time in the world to get into trouble. Mate, Ryan Giggs had the same amount of time on his hands, and he definitely earned more money than me. He didn't screw it up. I did, and that's because of the way that I was. I wanted to live my life like one of the lads,

Do Not Admit Defeat (the Day-to-Day Battle)

but I had one of those personalities that meant that once I got into something, like boozing or drugging, I couldn't stop.

I've been pretty clean ever since. I've relapsed on alcohol a few times, but I've never, ever, ever, not in a million years ever, gone back on to the drugs. Cocaine scared the shit out of me and I haven't touched it since that mad 10-month binge in 1994. It was that addictive, but it was never enjoyable. Coke was a waking nightmare.

I still gamble today, but I only play with amounts I can afford. These days, no bookie in the world will give me credit. Not after what I went through, it wouldn't look good. Everything happens for a reason, though. If I hadn't gambled all my money away, I'd be a multimillionaire today. The fact that I did means that I get to work on *Soccer Saturday* every weekend. It's just about the most fun thing I could imagine doing with my time. I honestly thought I had the best job in the world when I was a professional footballer – now I reckon I've got the second best. These days, I look forward to getting into the Sky studios as much as I looked forward to skinning defenders on a Saturday afternoon. Funny how things work out.

Looking back, I loved being a professional footballer in the late 1980s and early 90s, because it was fun. I could go out in the evening and do what I wanted and no one at Arsenal would ever know about it. Well, not really. They got those letters from fans and pub landlords, yeah, but there was nothing they could really pin on me. There were no phone cameras, so my face was never going to end up in the papers the next morning. I could get drunk, dance on the tables and no one would film it and post it on Facebook or Twitter. I had a licence to muck about.

The money wasn't great, but we played for the love of the game back then, so the pressure wasn't as bad. It was the perfect time to be a player. Not now. I saw Ledley King in the newspaper a few years ago, falling out of a night-club after Spurs had won the League Cup. He's a great footballer and he seems like a nice bloke. He'd had a night out after a day at Wembley and there were headlines all over the place because he'd celebrated hard. Believe me, when anyone comes out of those clubs, cameras flashing in front of them, it doesn't matter how sober they are, they always look paro. I should know, I've had it a million times.

Everyone went nuts over Ledley's night out, the fans and papers hammered him, but it was no different from what we were doing a couple of decades before. The only difference was that we were doing it a few times a week, every week. Those big nights are few and far between for top-drawer players now. Today, footballers live like saints compared to a lot of the people I played with.

It's the same on the pitch. The money's great now, don't get me wrong, but I just don't see the fun in football any more. I don't see the players laughing and joking; I

Do Not Admit Defeat (the Day-to-Day Battle)

don't see the refs laughing and joking. It's all very straight. I only have to look at the players' bodies these days to see how regimented everything is. They've got so much muscle it's scary. If I looked like that when I played, I'd have whipped my shirt off every five minutes, but then, half of the Premier League can't pass wind. Passing a ball from A to B makes you a good footballer, not having big pecs.

I admit it, though, I got lucky as a player. I won a lot of medals when, most of the time, I was off my head. The fact that I played for England after years of drinking and a serious drugging binge was a miracle in itself. I reckon that if I'd lived my life like one of the Straight Batters, I would have picked up a lorryload more caps. I don't have any regrets, though. If I worried about all the mistakes I'd made in life, I'd never get out of bed in the morning, but sometimes I do wonder, 'If I'd lived my life like Lee Dixon or Gary Lineker, could I have been as good as Glen Johnson?'

LESSON 20

Do Not Attempt to Pick a Worldy XI (Because It's the Hardest Job in the World)

1/ DAVID SEAMAN (ARSENAL, ENGLAND)

What a goalkeeper he was. I played with Peter Schmeichel for a couple of years when I was at Aston Villa, but he was coming to the end of his career at that time. When I played with Spunky at Arsenal, he was in his prime. There weren't many strikers who would look forward to coming up against him. If ever somebody broke through the Arsenal defence – which was pretty rare in those days – they then had to deal with the sight of him rushing off his goal line. No matter how good you were up front, Spunky would make the goal look double tiny because he knew his angles so well. If ever I scored against him in training from a one-on-one situation, I knew I'd done well.

He very rarely made a ricket, but when he did they tended to be goals that people remembered, like the Nayim goal against Arsenal in the 1995 UEFA Cup Winners' Cup Final against Real Zaragoza when he struck one over him from the halfway line, or the Ronaldinho free-kick in the 2002 World Cup when Brazil beat England. That one swerved over his head from a million miles out, too. People might look back at his career and think that he was prone to making mistakes with long-range shots, but I think they were freak goals that happened in two massive football matches. He didn't often get beaten from long distance when I played with him.

When it came to organising the defence, he was quiet – he wasn't a shouter or a screamer, he just got on with his job. We had Tony Adams to do the organising. Looking back, Spunky made so many great saves that he was nearly as important to Arsenal as somebody like Ian Wright at the other end of the pitch, but I've always said that the hardest thing in football is to put the ball into the back of the net, no doubt about that.

2/ GARY NEVILLE (MANCHESTER UTD, ENGLAND)

The best English right-back in my time. I've played with some great right-sided full-backs, like Lee Dixon for example, but Gary was an absolutely phenomenal player, an out-and-out defender. What really set him apart from a lot of the other full-backs I played with during my career was his positional play. I rarely saw him lose sight of the man he was marking. He wasn't one for napping at the back, either.

The other thing that struck me when I spent six weeks or so with him before and during the 1998 World Cup with England was just how professional he was. Like Paul Scholes and David Beckham - the other United lads in the international set-up who were also there - Gary wasn't one for messing around. Don't get me wrong, he would have a laugh with the lads, but I could tell he was determined to work as hard as he could when he was training or playing. I guess that's why he became the captain of Manchester United and not Mickey Mouse Rovers.

The understanding that he built up with David Beckham - both at international level and with United - was outstanding. I think David Beckham will look back on his career in years to come and realise that a big chunk of his success came about because he played with Gary Neville, and vice versa. They worked as a pair, not just up front, but in defence as well.

3/ KENNY SANSOM (ARSENAL, ENGLAND)

I made my debut when Kenny Sansom was playing for Arsenal, and he was always a great player in my eyes. People have short memories and they forget just how good he really was, but I remember when I was breaking into the first team under George Graham, I used to train with Kenny. Often I'd play against him in training, and I rarely got much change out of him.

Kenny, alongside Charlie Nicholas and Viv Anderson, would always help me out when I was cutting my teeth as a young player and they were all good pros. I say good pros – they were professional on the pitch, but they liked to have a good time off it as well.

To give you an idea of just how good Kenny Sansom was as a footballer, I've picked him over Stuart Pearce, who was a brilliant left-back for both Forest and England. I've also chosen him over Nigel Winterburn, who helped Arsenal to win all those trophies in the 90s. I just think that Kenny was a cut above. Forget the amount of caps that he got – and he picked up 86 between 1979 and 1988, appearing in the 1982 and 1986 World Cup finals in the process – he should have got a hell of a lot more. You have to remember that in those days there weren't a lot of international friendlies flying around. He would have got 120 caps if he had been playing today.

Like Gary Neville, he was all about defending. It's funny, I don't think that there are many full-backs like that these days, as funny as that sounds. Most of them are attacking right- and left-backs; they play like wingers most of the time. Micah Richards is probably the best defensive right-sided defender in the England frame at the moment, but going forward I can't think of anyone better than Kyle Walker and Glen Johnson, regardless of what he might think about me.

4/ PATRICK VIEIRA (ARSENAL, FRANCE)

He was a top-drawer central midfielder. As soon as Arsène Wenger signed him from AC Milan in 1996, the lads could all tell that he was going to be a fantastic player for us straightaway; after a month of being at the club Milan wanted to buy him back because they knew that they had made a massive ricket selling him.

What was great about Patrick was that he was tough, though the one thing I noticed when he arrived was that he was a very quiet lad to be around. That wasn't an indi- cation of how he was one the pitch because sometimes he used to win the midfield battle on his own, he was that tough. I always used to love watching Arsenal play Manchester United because some of the battles that Patrick had with Roy Keane were unbelievable. They used to kick lumps out of each other, but they were fair – Roy and Patrick were two top-class central midfielders and they both respected each other.

Patrick had everything: he could tackle, he could score goals and he could spot the killer pass. He had everything a top-class midfielder needs to do well in the Premier League, and he proved that by producing the goods in

World Cups for France and championships for Arsenal. It's very rare for a team to win anything without a world-class central midfielder and that's exactly what Patrick was. He was a big part of Arsène's success.

5/ TONY ADAMS (CAPTAIN) (ARSENAL, ENGLAND)

Tone was the leader of all leaders. England has John Terry these days, but I can't think of a centre-half in world football who leads the team out in the same way that Tony Adams did back then. He was an organiser, an inspiration and a footballer who would smash through a wooden door if his manager asked him to. He was a gaffer's dream – he'd dig players out in the dressing room if somebody wasn't pulling their weight, he'd have a go at someone if they weren't playing up to his standards. He would give everybody and anybody a rollicking if he wanted to and he wore his heart on his sleeve.

As a footballer, they didn't come much better than Tone; he was a proper centre-half. He was strong in the tackle, great in the air, composed on the ball and a great reader of the game. Like I mentioned before, he got ripped apart on his debut for Arsenal, and Marco van Basten ripped him apart during the 1988 European Championships when England played Holland, but that seemed to be the making of Tone. He bounced back a stronger player when a lot of other footballers would have been mentally ruined forever.

I suppose that was the thing that amazed me about Tone: he got better and better as he got older. Even when he came out of prison and admitted that he was an alcoholic, Tone seemed to improve and under Arsène Wenger he turned into a more technical player. That was summed up with his goal against Everton when Arsenal won the Premier League and FA Cup double in 1998 – Tone stormed the length of the pitch to score a last-minute goal in a 4–0 win. That was a great moment for him and it proved to me what a powerful force he was.

6/ DES WALKER (NOTTINGHAM FOREST, ENGLAND)

I very nearly picked Gareth Southgate for this because I played with him at Villa and I hadn't realised how good a footballer he was until I played in the same side as him. It's funny, with some lads you can tell that they're technically gifted, but it's not until you see them working alongside you, making your life easier, that you get an idea of just how talented they are. Gareth was exactly one of those players – a phenomenal centre-half, with no thrills or spills attached to him. He was always in control.

I've gone for Des Walker in my team because in the early 90s I thought he was one of the best central defenders in world football – I'd struggle to name many that were better. He was one of those defenders that I never really enjoyed playing against because he was so quick. If I'm picking Tone in the back four, I need someone with a bit of pace alongside him.

Des would generally manage to keep the centre-forward he was marking in his pocket during most games (though Ian Wright always seemed to score against him), but the one thing that stood him apart from some of the other defenders around at the time was that he was fair. He would never give you a kick. I always knew that on the rare occasions I went into a tackle with him I wasn't going to get hurt. Not like with Mick McCarthy. He was probably the hardest centre-half I ever came up against in my career, but a nice fella all the same.

7/ DAVID BECKHAM (MANCHESTER UTD, ENGLAND)

The best crosser of the ball I've ever seen. David could put the ball on a sixpence if he wanted to and he was a model pro. Whenever the lads weren't training under Glenn Hoddle for England during the 1998 World Cup, David would be out there practising his crosses and his free-kicks, often on his own for an extra half hour while the rest of us were waiting to get back to the team hotel. It was unbelievable to see. What he did on the football pitch wasn't down to luck; it all came from pure practice.

How Not To Be a Professional Footballer

When he was at Manchester United he was consistently playing at the top of his game. He would score important goals in big, big matches and sometimes, when United seemed to be under the cosh, he would pull out a top-drawer pass to set one of his team-mates up to score.

I think people thought he was just a right-winger, but there was more to his game than that. His movement was great, he could finish and his delivery from dead balls was amazing. I remember playing against him in the FA Cup when I was at Portsmouth. United got a free-kick outside the box and I stood in the Pompey wall. As David stepped up to take it, he shaped to shoot one way and then bent the ball the other way. It went straight into the top corner. I had to stop myself from applauding, that's how good it was.

He didn't do that once or twice, he scored goals like that all the time, but I didn't think that the goal he famously scored from the halfway line against Wimbledon in 1996 was as great as a lot of people made out, to be honest with you. I've always put goals into perspective. If that had happened at 0-0 with half an hour on the clock then, yeah, it would have been one of the best goals ever. But United were two up with next to no time left on the clock, so there was no danger really.

8/ PAUL GASCOIGNE (TOTTENHAM, ENGLAND)

The best English midfielder I've ever seen in my life, hands down. Gazza had everything. In 1990 he was the best player in football, and he was the star of the show at the World Cup in Italy that year. During Engand's game against Holland he ripped the Dutch to shreds single-handedly, and not many players could do that. It didn't really help us, mind, we only drew the game 0-0, but a lot of people thought we would get turned over in that game. I think the Dutch would say they were lucky not to lose it, especially after Gazza's performance.

I was fortunate enough to play alongside him a lot for Boro and for England, and watching him train was an absolute joy. He would pull off tricks and flicks that you wouldn't believe were possible. In practice games he would glide past three or four players in a flash and pop the ball over the goalie's head like it was the easiest thing in the world. He would embarrass people.

I played against him a few times and without question Gazza stopped Arsenal from winning the double in 1991 when he scored the first goal in that 3-1 defeat against Spurs in the FA Cup semi-final. For the first 25 minutes Gazza took the game by the scruff of the neck and we didn't have a chance of snatching it back. A lot of people – especially Spurs fans – go on about his 30-yard free-kick which rocketed past Spunky, but that wasn't the half of it.

For the opening half hour, Mickey Thomas – who wasn't a bad player either – couldn't get near to Gazza to win the ball back.

What I loved about playing with Gaz was that he could do something out of nothing. His skill and vision made it easier for me. Whenever he had the ball and I was playing in front of him, he would always look to pass it on. He was a team player. Sometimes footballers with that much skill want to do it on their own all the time and be the star of the show. Not Gaz. He was always looking to bring other people into play and win the game with the help of his team-mates.

9/ DENNIS BERGKAMP (ARSENAL, HOLLAND)

I didn't think a professional footballer could be that good, to be honest. When Dennis arrived at Arsenal he took the standard of training up tenfold: he would do flicks and passes that the lads couldn't believe; he would pull off an outrageous back heel or pluck the ball out of the air like it was a pillow before dinking it over the goalie's head. The rest of us would be speechless. We would look around at each other with our jaws open. I used to think, 'Hello, we've got some player here.'

In the first seven games or so at Arsenal, he couldn't score for toffee, but he was that good a player in training everybody knew that, when it finally clicked, the fans were going to see one of the best footballers to have ever put on an Arsenal shirt. And that's exactly what happened.

He was a very quiet lad, but he had a streak in him when he was on the pitch. If somebody upset him or if a defender kicked him about a bit, he would leave his foot in the next time the two of them came together. He wasn't a hard nut, don't get me wrong, but he was capable of putting himself about a bit when he needed to. He was a quiet assassin.

Vision in football is what some people call 'seeing the picture', realising in the mind how the game is going to unfold on the pitch before it actually happens. All the best players see the picture, but Dennis seemed to do it quicker than anyone I've ever played with. He was like a snooker player, constantly thinking two or three shots – or passes – ahead. That's what made him the best footballer I ever played with by a million miles.

10/ IAN WRIGHT (ARSENAL, ENGLAND)

This was a hard choice because I also played with Alan Shearer and Teddy Sheringham when I turned out for England, but I'm picking Wrighty because he was an out-and-out (and out-and-out) striker. He loved nothing more than to score goals, he was born to do it, and when he scored in training he would celebrate like it was the winning goal in a World Cup Final. Banging the ball into the back of the net made him so happy.

He wasn't a striker like Darren Bent is today – he didn't rely on service. I used to be able to pass the ball out to Wrighty on the halfway line and even if we were under pressure and he was surrounded by defenders, he could wriggle his way out of trouble and sprint into the opposition half before banging the ball past the keeper. He was lethal in a one-on-one situation. Alan Shearer was a brilliant centre-forward, but he didn't have that skill in his locker. That's what made Wrighty so special because scoring when you're one on one with the keeper, and you've got all that time to think, is one of the hardest things to do in football, at any level.

11/ DAVID ROCASTLE (ARSENAL, ENGLAND)

He wasn't left-footed but I want David in my team, and not just because he passed away so tragically in 2001. Rocky is in here on merit. He was a very, very good winger but an unusual winger at the highest level because he could tackle and he was hard as nails, which is rare in that position. David had everything in his game; he could score goals, make challenges, run rings round people and deliver excellent crosses. He was one of a kind.

I used to watch him dive in for 50–50 balls and wince. Half of the challenges he went into (and won) I wouldn't have fancied, thank you very much. In fact, I played on the wing for seven or eight years and I can't remember putting a tackle in once. I'd have rather ducked out of the way and not got hurt, but David was always up for the fight, and he would crunch people, but fairly. With the ball at his feet he was absolutely mesmerising.

I grew up with David. We were kids when we joined the Arsenal but I could tell he was a classy player from the minute I first started to kick around with him in the youth set-up. For me, it wasn't a surprise that David didn't get the caps he deserved because nothing surprised me in football when I played. The way the England squad was at the time meant that if you were in, then you would get 100 caps; if you weren't, it was nearly impossible for you to get a look in. It was a closed shop. At least, that's how it seemed to me. Look at Ian Wright, he should have played 10,000 times for England, but he had Alan Shearer and Teddy Sheringham in front of him. It was hard. Plus, England didn't play many friendlies in those days, so the chances of getting a game were slim.

It was a massive loss when Rocky died. I couldn't believe it when I heard. He was an absolute legend at Arsenal – he still is. And I'm a great believer that legends never die.

APPENDIX

Mersonisms – A *Soccer Saturday* Glossary

Beans on toast: The post; woodwork. 'He's only gone and hit the beans!' See also, 'The Sunday' (Sunday roast) and 'The Casper' (Casper the Friendly Ghost).

Cods: Codpiece; wedding tackle.

Dog and duck: Chalk and cheese; completely different. 'Rafa Benitez and Alex Ferguson are dog and duck.'

Fish up a tree, a: Clueless; of no use. 'Heurelho Gomes was like a fish up a tree in the Spurs goal today.'

Locker, in his: In his game. 'That Titus Bramble has a ricket in his locker.'

Lorryload: A lot.

Oner: One hundred quid.

Paro: Paralytic; drunk.

Pear: Pear-shaped; wrong.

Ricket: Mistake.

How Not To Be a Professional Footballer

Rocking horse shit: Rare; unusual. 'A Lee Dixon goal was like rocking horse shit.'

Silly o'clock: The early hours; way past bedtime.

The what'sname: General term for anything I've forgotten the name of.

Wax the dolphin: Masturbate; knock one out.

Worldy: World class. 'Joe Hart has pulled off a worldy there.'

Yankee: A type of bet. A wager on four horses or teams and consisting of 11 separate bets. That includes six doubles, four trebles and a fourfold accumulator. A minimum two selections must win to gain a return, not that I have many wins.